Expressive type today

Expressive type in
graphic design today

Compiled by
Counter-Print Books

n our fast-paced digital age, where attention spans wane and we are deluged with visual clutter, the power of expressive typography to command attention and provoke thought has never been more essential to design. Amidst the cacophony of competing voices clamouring for our attention, it is the designers who harness the full potential of type as a tool for expression who truly stand out from the crowd. They understand that typography is not simply a means of conveying information, but a potent form of visual rhetoric that can shape perceptions, evoke emotions and inspire action.

At the heart of expressive typography lies a spirit of playfulness and experimentation, an irrepressible urge to push boundaries, defy conventions and challenge the status quo. It is this spirit that infuses the work of the design agencies featured in this book, propelling them to new heights of artistic innovation. Whether it's through the use of unexpected materials, unconventional techniques, or daring juxtapositions of form and content, these designers fearlessly explore the limitless possibilities of typographic expression.

But expressive typography is not merely about breaking rules—it's about conveying meaning. It's about creating designs that resonate deeply with their audience, forging an emotional bond that transcends the boundaries of language and culture. It's about crafting narratives that speak directly to the soul, that convey a certain attitude, atmosphere or emotion.

As you flick through the pages of this book, we hope you enjoy the sheer diversity and richness of typographic expression today—the intricate interplay of form and space, the harmonious dance of colour and contrast, the exquisite balance of tension and space. But beyond the surface dazzle, take a moment to contemplate the deeper meaning embedded within each design—the stories told, the emotions conveyed and the ideas explored. ⬤

Jon Dowling

4

Moving type

Tokyo Dome City

○ Design: &Form
○ Web: andform.jp
○ Type: Custom.

&Form created a new identity design for Tokyo Dome City. This rebranding project includes the renovation of a wide range of facilities, including a baseball stadium, amusement parks, hot spring facilities, hotels, and theaters, spread across an expansive 135,000m².

&Form's design system is rooted in an original framework that maintains coherence while dynamically adapting to any aspect ratio and shape, seamlessly merging analogue and digital realms. This system produces a variety of visuals to enhance the entire complex and is supported by user-friendly software, ensuring ease of use. ●

'&Form's design system is rooted in an original framework that maintains coherence while dynamically adapting to any aspect ratio and shape, seamlessly merging analogue and digital realms.'

Skateyogi

○ Design:Order
○ Web: order.design
○ Type: Irregardless
   and Good Sans.

Skateyogi is a skateboard school based in Brooklyn, NY that offers camps, classes, and lessons to all age groups. Order created an identity that echoes the movement and expression found in skateboarding through typography. The vibrant, type-driven identity system celebrates the values of the Skateyogi community and captures their inclusive approach to learning. ●

'Order created an identity that echoes the movement and expression found in skateboarding through typography.'

SKATEYOGI

CULTURE.
CREATIVITY.
COMMUNITY.
RESPECT.
EXPRESSION.
FUN.
SKATING.

ska

SKATE

SKATEYOGI

SKATEYOGI

Register at skateyogi.com

Register at skateyogi.com

eVeRYONE CAN LEARN TO SKATE.

Skateboarding classes and camps for all ages.

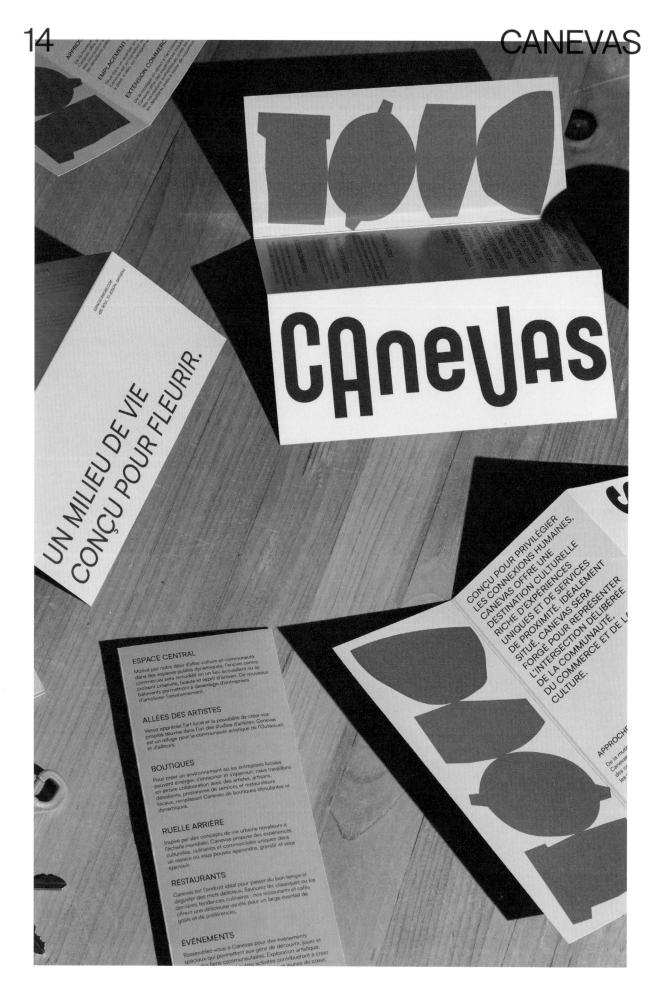

CaneVas

Canevas

○ Design: Philippe Clairoux
○ Web: clairouxstudio.com
○ Type: Logo—Custom.
   Other—Satoshi.

This colourful rebranding for the developer Brigil reflects the dynamic lifestyle of the Canevas project—a place where people are at the center of the community and where they can enjoy a variety of experiences.

    The brand treatment contains distinctive graphic forms that enrich the visual language and reflect the new energy of the space. A mix of abstract and more specific forms was designed to help reflect the concepts of the project and add be flexible to the brand. ●

Daniel Peter

HOW DID YOU BECOME INVOLVED IN GRAPHIC DESIGN?

As a teenager, I played in various bands and was fascinated by great record covers and concert posters. At some point, I wanted to design them too. I studied graphic design at the Lucerne School of Art and Design. After I graduated, we organised exhibitions in the fields of art, illustration and video in our studio space and held lectures and workshops. We designed posters and magazines for our events and did the scenography for the exhibitions. Those were my first jobs.

Since then, I have worked in various studios and for various offices in Switzerland and abroad. For several years now, I have been working in different constellations on various projects in several disciplines. I also teach at different design schools. O

CAN YOU SHARE YOUR PROCESS FOR DEVELOPING CONCEPTS AND SKETCHES WHEN STARTING A NEW PROJECT FOCUSED ON EXPRESSIVE TYPOGRAPHY? HOW DO YOU REFINE YOUR IDEAS TO ENSURE THEY EFFECTIVELY COMMUNICATE THE INTENDED MESSAGE OR EMOTION?

We focus on the customer, the project and the 'problem' to be solved. Even if the task is clearly defined, we try to take a step back to think about the project, the approach and the appropriate media. Once this process is complete, we start with broad thematic research and initial sketches. The ideas are condensed, simplified and summarised.

Once everything has been finalised in terms of content, we define rules that provide a fixed framework. Within the defined concept, we play with typography, shapes, colours and layout. O

CAN YOU SHARE A PROJECT WHERE YOU USED TYPOGRAPHY AS A PRIMARY MEANS OF EXPRESSION? WHAT MESSAGE OR EMOTION WERE YOU TRYING TO CONVEY, AND HOW DID YOU ACHIEVE IT THROUGH TYPOGRAPHY?

Typography is an important element in all our projects. We seek a conceptual and playful approach to it. For the Kofmehl project, typography becomes illustration or vice versa. For each poster, we design a typographic image in a defined space. We are completely free in the realisation, which makes the work very enjoyable. The only two rules for the design are: There is a clearly defined area and the subject is black on a coloured surface. All informative content is placed within a defined concept. O

△ Kulturfabrik Kofmehl.

'Even if the task is clearly defined, we try to take a step back to think about the project, the approach and the appropriate media. Once this process is complete, we start with broad thematic research and initial sketches.'

HOW DO YOU APPROACH THE PROCESS OF SELECTING TYPEFACES FOR PROJECTS THAT REQUIRE A STRONG EMOTIONAL OR EXPRESSIVE IMPACT? WHAT FACTORS DO YOU CONSIDER?

The choice of font is a design decision. A well-chosen font is important as it forms the basis of a project. It is important for us to work with well-drawn fonts. This is the only way to break through known conventions and find a playful approach. ○

EXPRESSIVE TYPOGRAPHY OFTEN INVOLVES BREAKING TRADITIONAL TYPOGRAPHIC RULES. HOW DO YOU STRIKE A BALANCE BETWEEN BREAKING CONVENTIONS AND ENSURING CLARITY AND EFFECTIVENESS IN COMMUNICATION?

We consider traditional typographic rules to be very important and are enthusiastic about the Swiss style. Conventional rules serve the purpose of clarity in communication. Swiss style means removing all emotion from the design and anonymising creativity. But we want to push the boundaries, try out daring things and fail in the process. We deliberately break typographic conventions and run the risk of compromising readability. ○

HOW DO YOU STAY INSPIRED AND CONTINUOUSLY PUSH THE BOUNDARIES IN YOUR DESIGN WORK? ARE THERE ANY SPECIFIC ARTISTS, MOVEMENTS, OR DESIGN TECHNIQUES THAT INFLUENCE YOUR CREATIVE PROCESS?

We value the exchange with our clients, friends from different design disciplines and design students. These contacts enable us to discover new ways of working and new ideas. For example, some time ago we organised the 'Pre Digital' exhibition at the Weltformat Graphic Design Festival. This showcased works that were created before the computer generation. Such content, contacts and design approaches are very inspiring.

In the design phase, we often experiment with manual techniques. We cut, glue, copy and scan. We are interested in the moment of chance and error. Our vision is to control, shape and elaborate on these until everything is just right. ○

HOW DO YOU MEASURE THE SUCCESS OF YOUR DESIGN WORK? CAN YOU PROVIDE EXAMPLES OF PROJECTS WHERE YOUR USE OF DESIGN HAD A SIGNIFICANT IMPACT ON THE AUDIENCE OR CLIENT OBJECTIVES?

We think it is very difficult to measure the influence of design. A good design for a bad project will not be successful. And vice versa as well. In order to achieve good projects, you first need good ideas and concepts, good content and constructive collaboration. ○

CAN YOU DISCUSS A PROJECT WHERE YOU USED UNCONVENTIONAL MATERIALS OR METHODS TO CREATE EXPRESSIVE TYPOGRAPHY?

We like to see typography as a geometric shape and play with it. We often work manually and also let chance play a part.

One project I can mention here is a concert poster for the Bad Bonn concert venue. The experiment of assembling the typography from countless individual parts worked well. But turning it into an animation was a lot of fun and the result is great. For us, continuing to work on projects and thinking outside the box is a method that takes us and the projects further. ○

DO YOU HAVE A FAVOURITE FONT AND WHY?

It depends on how we want to use the font. But we like the Neue Haas Grotesk. We appreciate its simplicity and the clear, simple shapes. It is timeless and versatile. The font was designed by Max Miedinger and Eduard Hoffmann in 1957. Later it was revised and became world-famous as Helvetica. Its minimalist design makes it easy to read and represents the Swiss style. ●

Kulturfabrik Kofmehl

○ Design: Studio DP
○ Web: herrpeter.ch
○ Type: Marfa.

Kulturfabrik Kofmehl is a venue for concerts, discos, readings, film nights and comedy events, as well as workshops, political panel discussions and theatre performances.

Studio DP was commissioned with the overall visual direction and, together with the venue's team, they developed a typographic and visual language that is minimalist and combines different languages and styles. Based on typographic images, they created a system to advertise the events. The concept offers Kulturfarbik endless possibilities for communicating its diverse content, programmes, events and messages in a targeted manner. ●

Project Send

O Design: Foreign Policy Design
O Web: foreignpolicy.design
O Type: Arial Narrow
　and Rublena Black.

Project Send's brand identity design and concept embody the gym's fundamental principles and distinctive approach of building the gym as a community of climbers. Every element, from the vibrant logotype to the fun copywriting, is meticulously crafted to encapsulate the essence of this climbing gym.

At the heart of the brand identity is the dynamic logotype, serving as a visual centerpiece. It captures the fluidity and energy inherent in climbing, representing the thrill and challenge that await within Project Send's walls.

The flexible identity system mirrors the multiple iterations and diverse directions encountered during climbing, symbolising the climbers' exploration of different paths and their determination to push boundaries and reach new heights. It serves as a visual reminder that success is not a linear progression but an ever-evolving journey of discovery.

With its dynamic identity and purposeful design, Project Send's brand identity conveys the exhilaration, adventure, and constant evolution that define the climbing experience. It serves as a visual representation of the gym's core values, inspiring climbers to embrace challenges, defy limits, and embark on a transformative journey toward personal growth and achievement. ●

My Other Life

○ Design: Simin Xu
○ Web: behance.net/siminxbs
○ Type: Owners Narrow.

This creative scented candle series, titled 'My Other Life', is inspired by love, freedom, and travel—a concept connecting time and space. Simin Xu tried to use the design and packaging to convey the state of time travel. The colourful circular gradient is like an open door to time and space, and the 'door' of the inner box is subtly presented in a hollowed out way. The inner box adopts a monochrome, high-contrast design. Open the box cover and the third layer is a deeper black, which is used to set off the metal texture and colour of the product.

A set of glyphs was designed for this series. The slanted and dynamic forms inject a free and casual personality into the text. The stickers of the six scents are designed in a differentiated way, using graphics and colours to add to the My Other Life visual language. ●

'The slanted and dynamic forms inject a free and casual personality into the text.'

MY OTHER LIFE
PEONY PAVILION
WHISPER IN THE FOREST
TO THE LIGHTHOUSE
CHANT AT POLAR
FIRE OF LOVE
UNTIL THE END
SCENTED CANDLE
SERIES
KEEP LOVING,
KEEP FREE
6 IN 1
XGIMI
寓义 TO DEFINE

Stiftung Mercator Schweiz

○ Design: Raffinerie
○ Web: raffinerie.com
○ Type: Helvetica.

The visual identity of Stiftung Mercator Schweiz is all about change. This reflects the mission of the Swiss foundation. The dynamically growing and moving line symbolises Mercator's philosophy of co-creating, experimenting, learning and sharing knowledge to initiate change for the common good. The use of bold colours and playful typography underlines the foundation's open and courageous mindset to break new ground while tackling the challenges of our time. ●

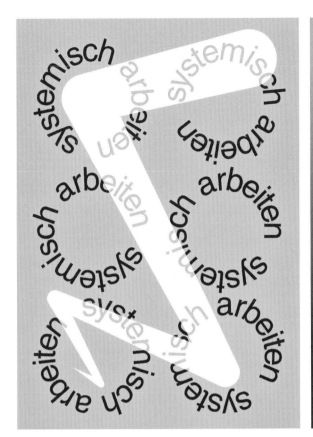

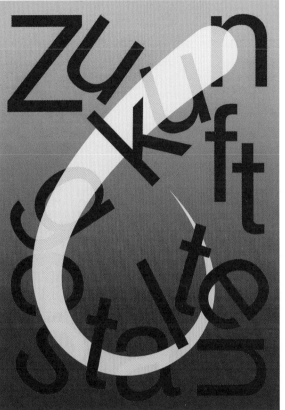

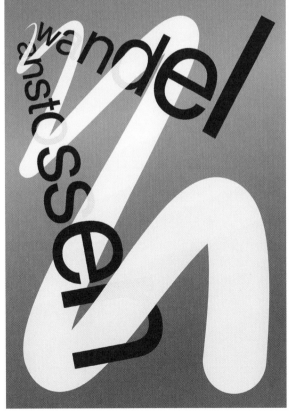

systemisch arbeiten

Allia

Ideen entwickeln

Zukunft gestalten

systemisch arbeiten

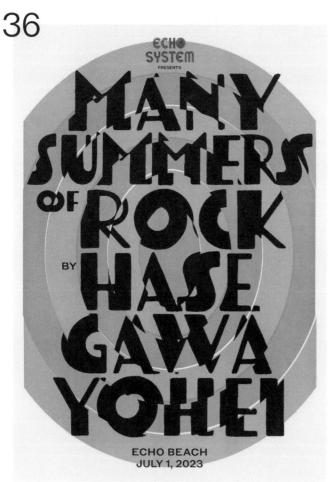

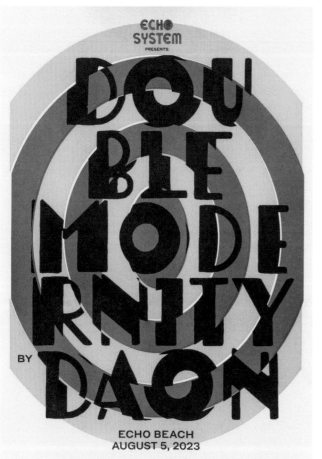

'The posters drew inspiration from the dynamic concentric circles in Echo's logo. These circles represent the radiant sun and embody the Jamaican sound system that amplifies the pulsating energy of summer music.'

Echo Beach

○ Design: Studio fnt ○ Web: studiofnt.com ○ Type: Tomarik Display.

After its successful launch in 2022, Echo Beach came back for its second year.
Every weekend until August, the vibrant beats of various DJs took over this paradise,
creating the ultimate summer music experience. As the designers in charge,
Studio fnt were responsible for creating the captivating Echo Beach poster series for
2023. The posters drew inspiration from the dynamic concentric circles in Echo's logo.
These circles represent the radiant sun and embody the Jamaican sound system that
amplifies the pulsating energy of summer music. ●

Too Much To Watch

O Design: Kiln
O Web: studio-kiln.com
O Type: Title – Custom. Other – Lay Grotesk.
O Photography: Richard Kendal.

The RTS's annual event brings industry leaders together to discuss the future of media. 2023's event, Inspired by the title of this year's event, Studio Kiln created an identity that playfully explored the idea of a crowded screen. Each letter, word and phrase competes for our attention; imitating the dizzying array of content viewers have to navigate.

The identity had to adapt to multiple touchpoints with the balloon-like letters inflated to fill screens, book covers, windows and pillars; creating a delightfully overwhelming experience for attendees. ●

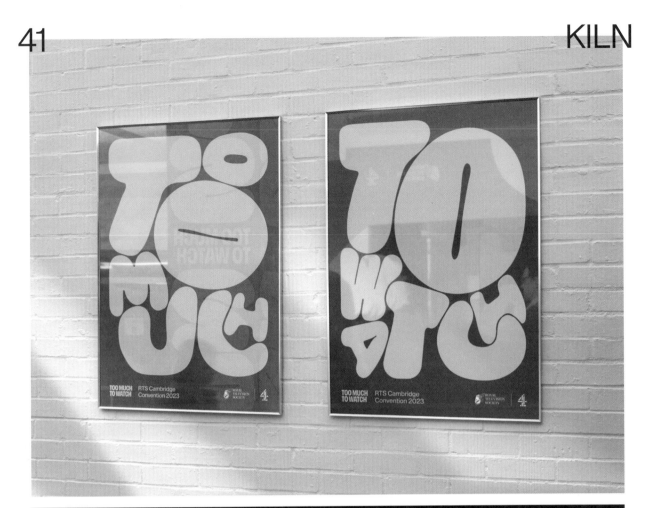

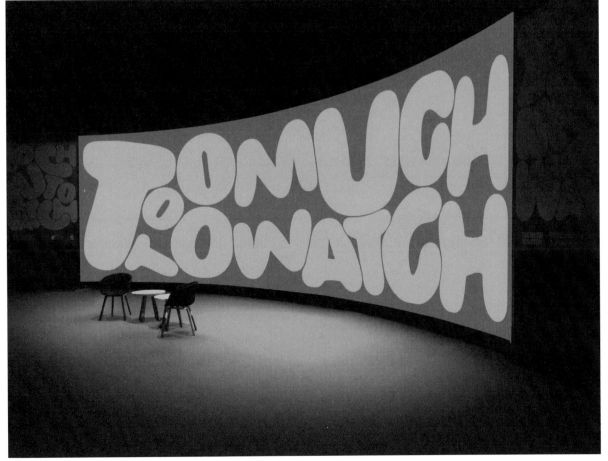

Illustrative type

'The typographic illustrations represent song names that ignited positive social movements.'

Grams

O Design: TNOP Design
O Web: tnop.com
O Type: Custom and Poppins.

This packaging series for Grams, a medical and exotic-grade cannabis dispensary in Bangkok, prioritises user education on safe usage and delivering high-quality products.

Inspired by the brand's concept of 'The Creation', TNOP Design developed the theme of 'The Inspiring Change' for the packaging design. The typographic illustration represents song names that ignited positive social movements.

The design includes cannabis containers in four sizes, featuring a double-layered PET inside and PP outside for optimal storage, and a versatile shopping bag/delivery box for secure sealing. Through this packaging, Grams aims to offer top-notch products while promoting responsible consumption and societal progress. ●

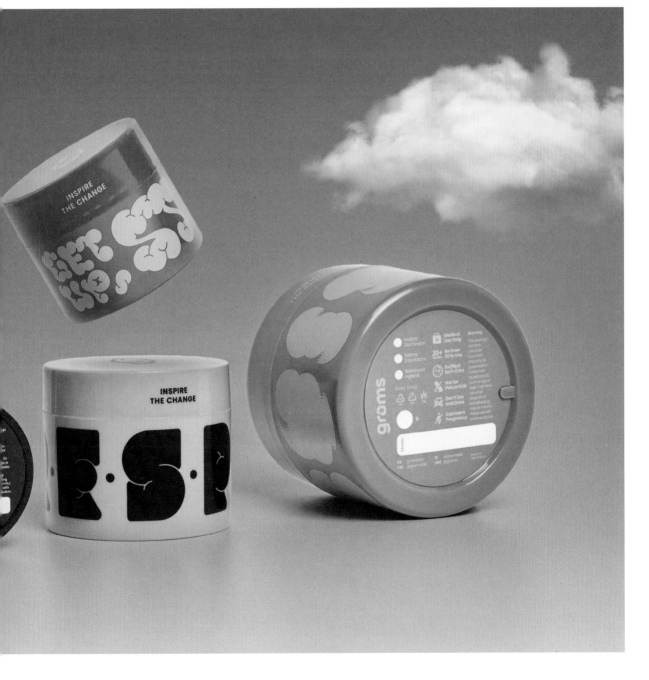

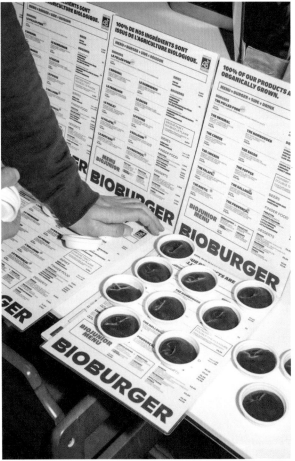

Bioburger

○ Design: Abmo
○ Web: abmo.fr
○ Type: Logo and Emojis—Custom. Other—BB Ginto Nord Regular, BB Ginto Nord Condensed Black and BB Ginto Regular Bold.

Created in 2011, Bioburger is the pioneer of 100% organic fast food in France. Its old visual identity did not sufficiently convey the deliciousness of the offering, nor the commitment behind the recipes and choice of suppliers. Abmo proposed a new, very assertive, sincere and lively visual identity. A bold, appetising and cheerful logo suggests a smile and a burger. A new bright orange colour gives impact and visibility to the brand and distinctive, contemporary typography composes catchy, gently playful messages.

    With this new visual identity, Biobuger is taking a new step in its development to involve more and more people in the societal transition around a product loved by all. ●

'A bold, appetising and cheerful logo
suggests a smile and a burger.'

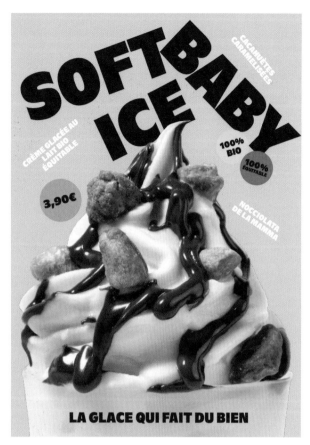

BB EMOJIS

Mama Mexa

○ Design: Seachange
○ Web: seachange.studio
○ Type: Custom.

Mama Mexa is a vibrant new pop-up taqueria offering healthy fast food inspired by Mexican markets. The brand identity celebrates Mexico's colourful culture through a bespoke, flamboyant wordmark resembling blooming flowers. This distinctive typeface, complete with decorative glyphs, pays homage to Mexican flora and fauna, avoiding clichés of typical Mexican eateries.

Each letter features varying width petals, exuding an eccentric energy. The wordmark can be abbreviated to 'M' for scalability and is complemented by a typeface evoking traditional Mexican motifs. This unique approach ensures instant brand recognition while refreshing the portrayal of Mexican culture in the culinary scene. ●

Awakening

○ Design: Studio fnt
○ Web: studiofnt.com
○ Type: Custom.

The Seoul International Writers' Festival (SIWF) is a global literary event that expands opportunities to appreciate literature and fosters international exchange. The SIWF in 2021 aimed to reflect on and embrace the profound changes brought about by the pandemic. It acknowledged that crises and hardships originate from human actions, and our collective responsibility is to overcome them.

Through this festival, Studio fnt strove to raise awareness and strengthen the audience's collective resolve to start anew. In their design, they sought to convey that the concept of 'Awakening' extends beyond individual introspection. It represents a collective awakening, encouraging everyone to contemplate the impact of literature on today's world. To convey these abstract concepts, Studio fnt incorporated sparkling patterns that rotate within the alphabet, symbolising this year's theme and the event's vibrancy. ●

자각 - Awakening

2021 서울국제작가축제
Seoul International
Writers' Festival
10. 8. – 24.
www.siwf.or.kr

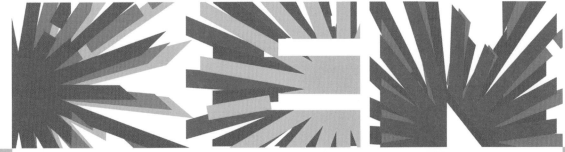

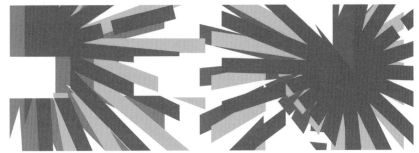

National Repertory Season

○ Design: Studio fnt ○ Web: studiofnt.com ○ Type: Custom.

Founded in 1950, the National Theater of Korea has been a leader in art performances in Korea for over 60 years. National Repertory Season is an annual program presenting innovative new works and the best repertoire by national arts groups in theater, traditional drama, dance, and orchestra. The visual concept of the National Repertory Season 2019—2020 was 'fireworks'. Fireworks are the elements making up the National Theater of Korea logo and can be used as components to express a festive mood. Also, by connecting the lines of the fireworks and utilising four different colours, Studio fnt were able to make the letters of the title into a vivid image. ●

Zoncello

○ Design: Swear Words
○ Web: swearwords.com.au
○ Type: Logo—Custom. Other—GT Pressura Mono.
○ Photography: Northbrook Agency.

Featuring zesty yellows, playful effervescence and stripes these packaging designs are an ode to the Italian Riviera.

A suite of products from Yarra Valley's Zonzo Estate, Zoncello & Zoncello Spritz are made with owner Rod Micallef's delicious Limoncello recipe featuring local lemons and a base spirit made from Zonzo Estate's grapes. ●

○ Abmo
○ Jesús López
○ Blurr Bureau
○ Reesaw
○ Studio Furious
○ DE_FORM
○ Universal Favourite
○ Olympic Studio
○ Lukas Diemling
○ Monozygote
○ Mother Design

Curvy type

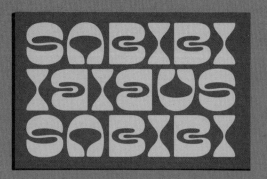

Sabibi

○ Design: Abmo ○ Web: abmo.fr ○ Type: Logo—Custom. Other—GT Ultra and Helvetica.

Sabibi is the contraction of sandwich and habibi, which means 'my love, my darling' in Arabic and Hebrew. Sabibi is an ode to diversity and fraternity. This is the promise of a rich and creative culinary journey to the heart of the Mediterranean, from Athens to Beirut, via Tel Aviv and Damascus. For this feel-good pita counter, Abmo imagined a warm, generous and playful visual identity. A curvy, vintage-inspired logo design, striking expressive typography, sunny colours, and gourmet iconography. ●

**Sandwichs Pain Pita
Street Food Levantine**

11 rue du Canal - Rennes
+33 (0)6 12 34 56 78

MENUS

Pita ou Bowl	9.00€	Pita ou Bowl + accompagnement	12.00€	Pita ou Bowl + accompagnement + dessert	14.50€
Pita du moment	10.00€	Pita ou Bowl + accompagnement + boisson	14.00€	Pita ou Bowl + accompagnement + boisson + dessert	15.00€

SANDWICHS PITA

PITA CHICHE

Houmous paprika fumé
Salade chou rouge menthe concombre citron confit
Confit oignons carottes et mélasse de grenade
Falafels Sauce mangue fenugrec
Amandes caramélisées miel et zaatar
Pickles à l'aneth Feta, Persil, Grenade

PITA MAMI

Babaganoush (caviar d'aubergine)
Salade chou rouge menthe concombre citron confit
Confit oignons carottes et mélasse de grenade
Halloumi pané
Sauce betterave, rose et mélasse de grenade
Amandes caramélisées miel et zaatar
Pickles à l'aneth Feta, Persil, Grenade

PITA SHOUSHOU

Houmous citron confit
Salade chou rouge menthe concombre citron confit
Confit oignons carottes et mélasse de grenade
Beignets de légumes, cannelle
Sauce persil nigelle
Amandes caramélisées miel et zaatar
Pickles à l'aneth Feta, Grenade

PITA DU MOMENT

Houmous
Salade chou blanc, pruneaux, piment d'espelette
Confit oignons carottes et mélasse de grenade
Beignets de légumes, cannelle
Sauce cacao, poivre
Pignons grillés
Pickles Feta, Persil, Grenade

BOWLS

Mêmes recettes que les sandwichs mais
avec une base de lentilles (sans pain)

DESSERTS   3.50€

Cookies fleur d'oranger chocolat blanc
Gâteau chocolat tahini
Fromage blanc, fruits frais, huile d'olive, miel

SIDES   3.50€

Potatoes
Patate douce rôtie
→ Sauce sésame / Sauce sésame harissa forte
Coleslaw de chou blanc, pomme, carotte, aneth
→ Mayo tahini + Oxitoro de reste de Pita

(Option) : Petit pot de pickles

BOISSONS

Eau plate	2.00€
Eau Gazeuse	4.00€
Coca	2.00€
Ice tea	4.00€
Orangina	2.00€
Jus préssé	4.00€

Eau plate	2.00€
Eau Gazeuse	4.00€
Coca	2.00€
Ice tea	4.00€
Orangina	2.00€
Jus préssé	4.00€

'The fresh and relaxed qualities they live by are represented in the style of the logotype. The brand conveys a unique, fun, Mexican, crafty feeling and at the same time, something slightly retro and groovy.'

Mentados

○ Design: Jesús López ○ Web: jesuslopez.co ○ Type: Blimey, Hobo, Nouveau Hippie, Carters, Saa Series, Moskau Grotesk, Carlsbad and Retrips.

Mentados is a company that produces fermented and carbonated drinks. They're based in northern Mexico, in Hermosillo, Sonora. The first flavour they launched is the original fermented and carbonated kombucha, although they also experiment with other flavours, such as Jamaica (hibiscus). They prioritise the search of what is pleasant to the senses without taking themselves too seriously. The fresh and relaxed qualities they live by are represented in the style of the logotype. The brand conveys a unique, fun, Mexican, crafty feeling and at the same time, something slightly retro and groovy. ●

"ME RINDO"
-EL CALOR
(NO TIENE OPORTUNIDAD
CONTRA LA MENTADA FRESCURA)

✳ LOS *Mentados* REFRESCOS ✳

Flings

○ Design: Blurr Bureau
○ Web: blurrbureau.com
○ Type: Garnett Black, Quick Brush
   and Agrandir Text Bold.

Flings is the brainchild of two fun-loving founders who have brought in a new era of toaster pastries. Blurr Bureau led the way from the brand's inception to final execution, working on everything from market research, strategy, naming, tone of voice, visual identity, packaging, website and typography.

   Inspired by the essence of nostalgia, Flings transports adult snackers to a time before the digital age. The custom calligraphy of the Flings brand mark was designed to mimic frosting and ooze juicy appetite appeal, with the additional typefaces chosen to highlight and compliment the brand's playful and cheeky nature. ●

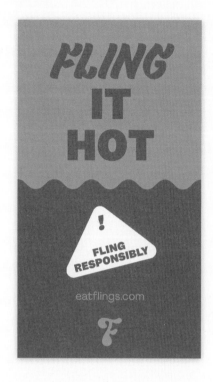

GUNCI

○ Design: Reesaw
○ Web: reesaw.com
○ Type: Cheee-Shishi.

In the Chinese context, 'GUN' means to maintain a boiling state. GUNCI has an inherent restless temperament, so Reesaw hoped to incorporate plenty of emotional expression into the design.

In the design of the Chinese font, they added exaggerated glyph features to simulate the effect of liquid, and chose the English font Cheee-Shishi, with the same characteristics, to be used together. This typographic visual system created a flowing visual experience, just like a heatwave coming, presenting a fiery, fun brand image. ●

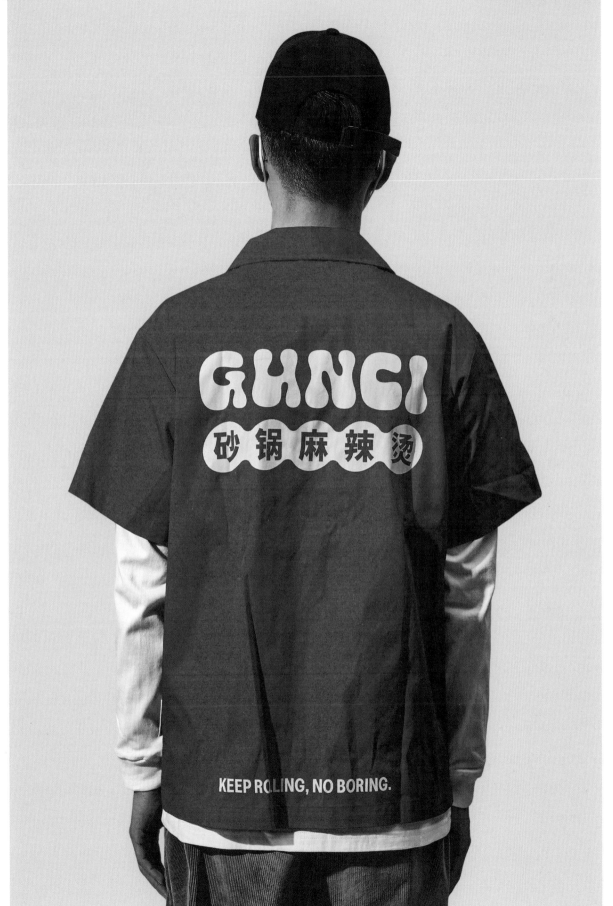

Quentin Weisbuch

HOW DID YOU BECOME INVOLVED IN GRAPHIC DESIGN?

Actually, I didn't think I would become a graphic designer at the beginning of my student life. I wanted to be a product designer, then I studied packaging design and after two or three internships, I ended up in graphic design and I loved it! ○

CAN YOU SHARE YOUR PROCESS FOR DEVELOPING CONCEPTS AND SKETCHES WHEN STARTING A NEW PROJECT FOCUSED ON EXPRESSIVE TYPOGRAPHY?

When I start a branding project, I always try a lot of different fonts before selecting three to five of them that offer the right emotion. My approach in developing concepts is always related to the idea of giving sense to my graphic choices. And I'm always willing to be able to justify my proposal. ○

CAN YOU SHARE A PROJECT WHERE YOU USED TYPOGRAPHY AS A PRIMARY MEANS OF EXPRESSION? WHAT MESSAGE OR EMOTION WERE YOU TRYING TO CONVEY?

The Goblet project is one of the branding identities that uses typography as a primary means of expression. With its super rounded and curved shapes, the Cheee font drives you directly into a psychedelic and fuzzy world. That's what I wanted to evoke, in reference to the crazy cocktail recipes Goblet is putting in its bottles. ○

△ Goblet.

HOW DO YOU APPROACH THE PROCESS OF SELECTING TYPEFACES FOR PROJECTS THAT REQUIRE A STRONG EMOTIONAL OR EXPRESSIVE IMPACT? WHAT FACTORS DO YOU CONSIDER?

I think it's a question of feeling moreover if the idea is to convey an emotion. Sometimes you can't explain why but the typeface fits perfectly to the project. ○

EXPRESSIVE TYPOGRAPHY OFTEN INVOLVES BREAKING TRADITIONAL TYPOGRAPHIC RULES. HOW DO YOU STRIKE A BALANCE BETWEEN BREAKING CONVENTIONS AND ENSURING CLARITY AND EFFECTIVENESS?

It depends on the project, sometimes having fun with typography, while mixing super-different fonts together can be hilarious, even when it's over exaggerated. For example, one of my brand identity projects, named Rolls (spring roll restaurant in Paris), uses three or four different typefaces together.

I got inspired by vintage Asian restaurant signage in Paris and around the world, that used to mix a lot a different fonts to create ugly designs that today look kind of cool (maybe because it reminds us of childhood memories).

'When I start a branding project, I always try a lot of different fonts before selecting three to five of them that offer the right emotion. My approach in developing concepts is always related to the idea of giving sense to my graphic choices. And I'm always willing to be able to justify my proposal.'

And on the other hand, I sometimes play with typefaces on a more modest scale. For example, in the Goblet project I vertically stretched the typeface to fit to the bottle size. But shhhhh, please don't tell Oh No Type! ○

△ Rolls.

HOW DO YOU STAY INSPIRED AND CONTINUOUSLY PUSH THE BOUNDARIES IN YOUR DESIGN WORK? ARE THERE ANY SPECIFIC ARTISTS, MOVEMENTS, OR DESIGN TECHNIQUES THAT INFLUENCE YOUR CREATIVE PROCESS?

personally like to get inspired by pictures of fonts used in projects, rather than spending time scrolling on the websites of type foundries. ○

CAN YOU DISCUSS A PROJECT WHERE YOU USED UNCONVENTIONAL MATERIALS OR METHODS TO CREATE EXPRESSIVE TYPOGRAPHY?

The Rolls brand identity is definitely one of the projects I had the most fun with—designing the posters, signage or leaflets, with almost no typographic rules. As I mentioned previously, the Rolls branding is inspired by vintage Chinese takeaway restaurants and their home-made menus and signage. My goal was to make cool graphic designs with this unconventional typography inspiration. ○

DO YOU HAVE A FAVOURITE FONT AND WHY?

absolutely love Adobe Garamond Condensed Light. I think this is perhaps because it is reminiscent of vintage Apple Macintosh advertising. ○

WHAT ARE YOUR GOALS FOR THE FUTURE OF YOUR COMPANY?

'd like to be able to increase the number of projects that can mix different types of expression: photography, typography, motion, product design, film etc. ●

Goblet

○ Design: Studio Furious
○ Web: studiofurious.com
○ Type: Logo—Customised
   Juanito. Other—Neue Haas
   Grotesk.

Goblet is a takeaway cocktail brand located in Paris, France. The brand identity was designed by Quentin Weisbuch (Studio Furious). Weisbuch used Cheee by OH no Type Co. in Juanito. For the logotype he made a custom, compressed version of the Juanito version to fit to the size of the bottle. The typeface, with its super- rounded shapes, is an analogy to the distortion of vision while drinking alcohol. For the body text, he worked with a Roman weight from Neue Haas Grotesk by Christian Schwartz. ●

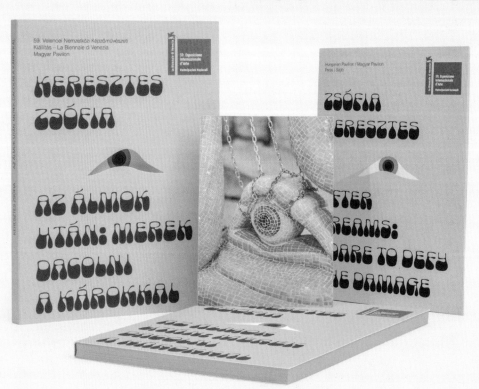

Zsófia Keresztes

○ Design: DE_FORM
○ Web: de-form.hu
○ Type: Cheee Conshred and Cheee Bingbong.

The 59th Venice Biennale's Hungarian Pavilion showcased Zsófia Keresztes' solo exhibition, 'After Dreams: I Dare to Defy the Damage' in 2022.

The exhibit delves into the complex interplay between past, present, and future, navigating identity through four thematic units. Following its stint in Venice, the showcase moved to Budapest's Ludwig Museum.

The graphic design centers on the artist's recurring motif, the eye, mirroring the sculptures' hues. The chosen typography echoes the objects' distinctive shapes, creating a cohesive visual identity that harmonises with the exhibition's exploration of time and self. ●

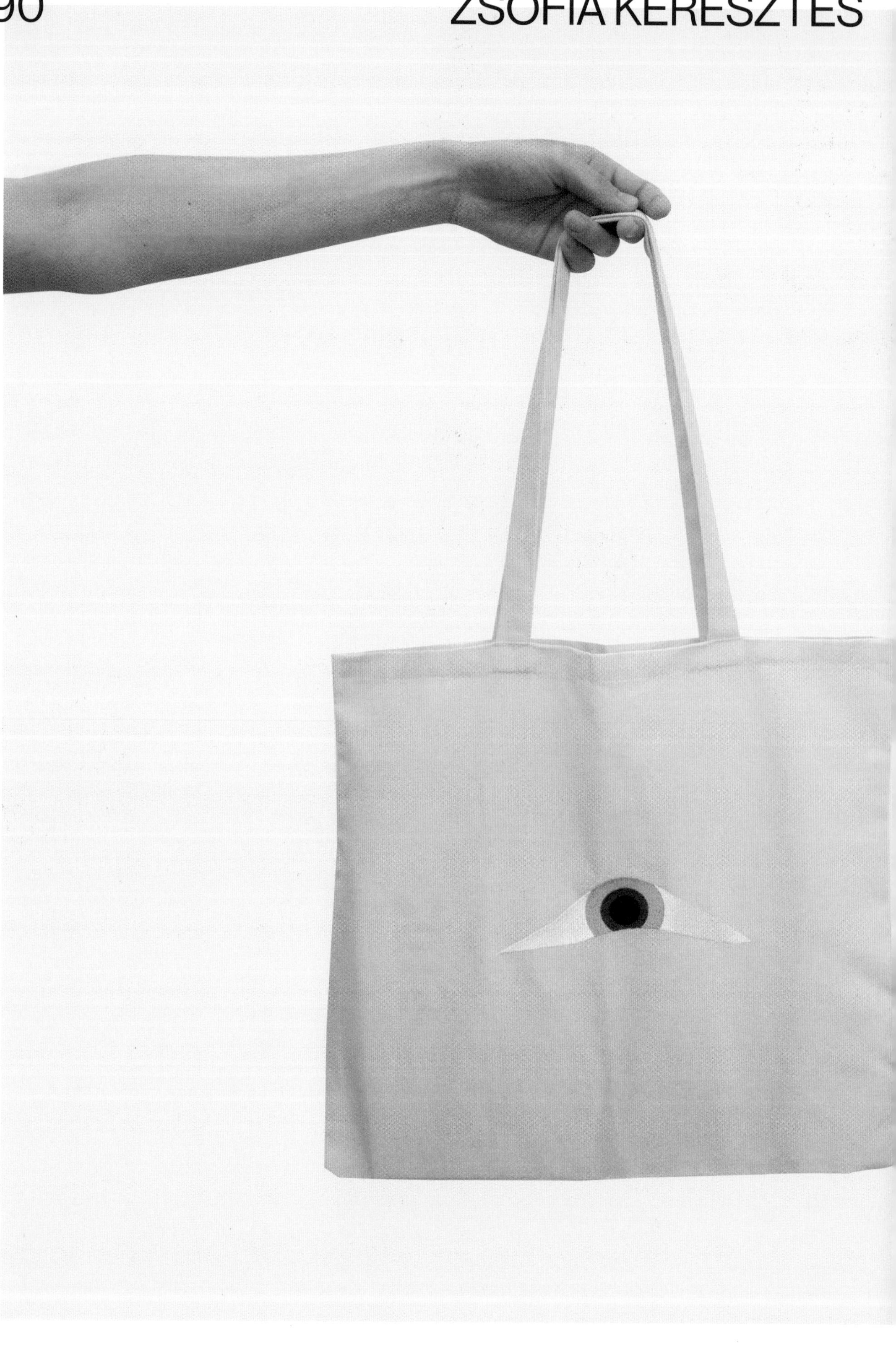

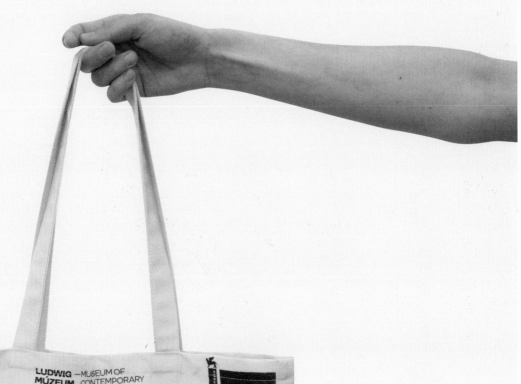

Flaus

○ Design: Universal Favourite ○ Web: universalfavourite.com.au
○ Type: Logo—Customised from Cheee. Other—Founders Grotesk X Condensed
and Untitled Sans.

Flaus is reimagining the oral healthcare space, starting with the world's first planet-friendly electric flosser. Flaus wanted to create a brand that would bring flossing into the 21st century but also rise above the swathe of superficial and 'trendy' millennial brands emerging as part of the oral beauty boom. This meant bringing their environmental ethos to the front without falling into stale 'eco' tropes or the blur of brands saying the same meaningless things. Heavily influenced by the retro-futuristic brand direction, the logo is a customised quip on Cheee from OH no Type Co., with both the 'A' and the 'U' taking the shape of teeth. Its chubby, expressive character challenges the category norms of clean, sans serif and subtle typefaces, signifying the brand's distinct difference in the oral beauty space. ●

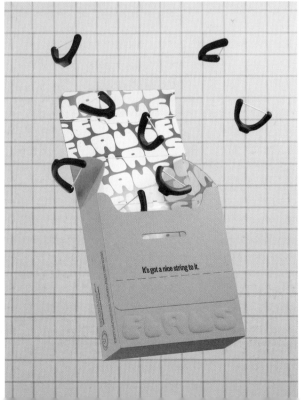

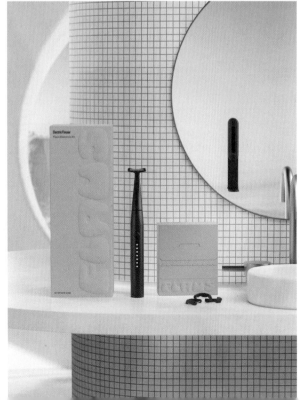

FLAUS

Mind the gaps

Keep your mouth happy and mind the gaps with Flaus — the electric flosser as gentle on your gums as it is on the planet.

GOFLAUS.COM

TOSS THE FLOSS

PEN UP
TO A
ETTER
RLD OF
AL CARE.

Floss for the future.

Get Flaus.

Gross by nature,
good by the earth.

In this house we Flaus

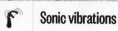

Sonic vibrations

Waterproof (IP67)

Planet friendly

OddWorks

○ Design: andstudio
○ Web: andstudio.lt
○ Type: Logo—Custom. Other—Neue Haas Grotesk.

OddWorks is a subscription-based, cold brew, coffee brand. Founded by two friends, they manifest that 'odd' can actually work, and something that is unusual can be appealing. OddWorks needed to stand out from the category to change coffee lovers' perspectives on daily consumption.

　　Graphically, andstudio conveyed this through the brand's energetic look, where letters and symbols become distorted and fit into a layout. Somehow 'odd' becomes intriguing, inviting everyone to question what the brand is about. ●

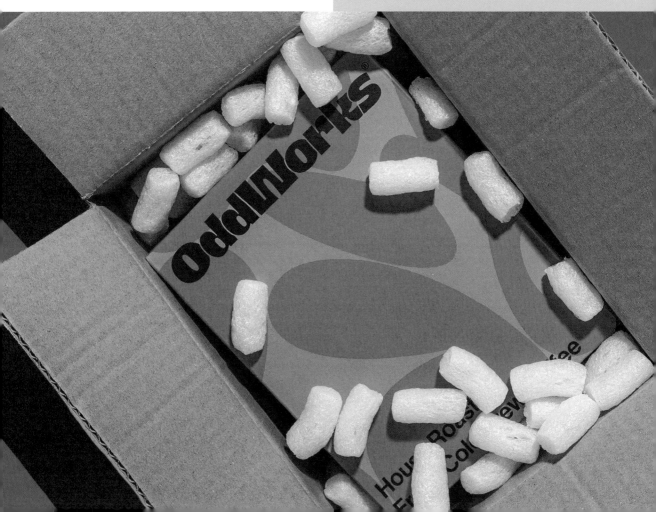

Mesmerised & Energized

Mesmerised & Energized

Cold brew doesn't use heat to extract the good stuff, it uses time! Cold brewing takes between 12-24 hours to properly extract. We think it's on another level to standard iced coffee. The difference is obvious when you cold brew.

The Fresh Cold Brew Company

Fresh Coffee Company

The Fresh Cold Brew Company

Fresh & Delicious

Cold brew doesn't use heat to extract the good stuff, it uses time! Cold brewing takes between 12-24 hours to properly extract. It's on another level to standard iced coffee. Cold brew highlights the difference between coffee and roast

Fyr

○ Design: Olympic Studio ○ Web: olympicstudio.fr ○ Type: Bota and Area.

To promote alternatives to conventional sodas, addressing significant health and environmental concerns, Olympic Studio imagined Fyr, a water kefir brand. The aim of Fyr was to offer a simple beverage derived from an ancient process, with the potential for various surprising and sophisticated flavours. Beginning with the creation of a lively logo depicting the natural process of kefir production, the final result features joyful and peculiar organic shapes that captivate attention. Subsequently, they developed labels with a tranquil and soothing design, contrasting the energy of the logo and distinguishing the brand from the noisy world of traditional sodas. ●

Grazer Impro Fest

○ Design: Lukas Diemling
○ Web: diemling.com
○ Type: Pilowlava and Founders Grotesk.

In August 2023, Schaumbad—Freies Atelierhaus Graz became a utopian resort for the first Grazer Impro Fest. Over nine days, artists and collectives converged to improvise together, explore singing, making instruments, cooking and networking.

Lukas Diemling was asked to develop an identity and poster design reflecting the festival's uniqueness, while conveying essential information. Utilising Founders Grotesk and Pilowlava typefaces, he created a typographic blend symbolising improvisation. From Pilowlava, a vibrant key visual emerged, embodying the festival's diversity and playfulness. This graphic system extended to posters, flyers, and both analogue and digital mediums. ●

CONCERTS
WORKSHOPS,
PERFORMANCES
LECTURES
AND TALKS

SCHAUMBAD EDITION 01   25. AUG — 2. SEP 23

COFFE

WE
DON'T
GIF A
FUCK

'Lukas Diemling was asked to develop an identity
and poster design reflecting the festival's uniqueness,
while conveying essential information.'

Friss

O Design: Monozygote
O Web: studiomonozygote.com
O Type: Herbus and Neue Montreal.

Monozygote crafted the visual identity and packaging for Friss to help the product stand out among competitors on supermarket shelves. Adopting a playful yet clean aesthetic, they departed from conventional graphic norms associated with 'granola' products, using the Herbus typeface by Elliot Grunewald and Neue Montreal from Pangram Pangram. Despite a monochromatic base, the packaging transforms into a vibrant world of colourful stripes and chequered textures. The objective is to create an interchangeable system facilitating integration of different flavours or partnerships while maintaining visual consistency and a strong brand identity. ●

'Despite a monochromatic base, the packaging transforms into a vibrant world of colourful stripes and chequered textures.'

PARK LANE

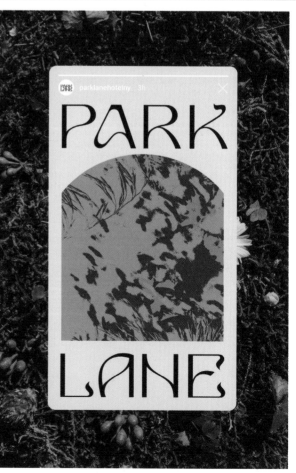

Park Lane

○ Design: Mother Design
○ Web: motherdesign.com
○ Type: Logo—Custom. Other—Folio.

The Park Lane Hotel in New York City is an only-of-its-kind, uptown sanctuary situated prominently on Central Park South. Boasting 47 stories of magnificent views, the newly renovated hotel sought to stand apart from the exclusionary, old-world luxury of Billionaire's Row surrounding it.

For its new brand identity and wordmark, Mother Design drew inspiration from the hotel's new interiors, unique architecture, and location along the park. Meandering lines, like wandering paths, taper off into whimsical, ornate flairs that resemble botanical tendrils—organic elements that are contrasted with contemporary, straight lines harkening back to the hotel's iconic facade. ●

LET'S RAMBLE,
YOU AND I

1 2 3 4 5
6 7 8 9 0

Serif type

'A key aspect of the design studio's endeavor was crafting a graphic identity that captured its historic essence while heralding a new era.'

Masvell

○ Design: Ingrid Picanyol Studio
○ Web: ingridpicanyol.com
○ Type: Bonaventura Regular.

Rescuing El Mas Vell's extraordinary history, Ingrid Picanyol Studio embarked on renewing its beachside haven while reviving its intimate relationship with Masnou's people. A key aspect of the design studio's endeavor was crafting a graphic identity that captured its historic essence while heralding a new era. Collaborating with typographer Noe Blanco, they meticulously designed a custom typeface inspired by architect Bonaventura Bassegoda's calligraphy. This font, an elegant yet dynamic creation, seamlessly integrates into their modular graphic system. It's a homage to El Mas Vell's iconic heritage, respecting its architectural environment by incorporating traditional elements and seamlessly blending modernity with tradition. ●

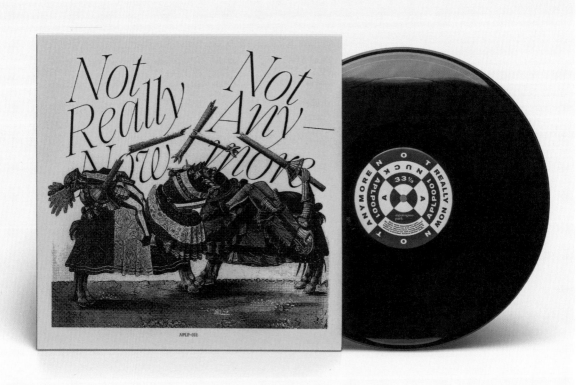

NUCK—Not Really Now Not Anymore

○ Design: Studio fnt
○ Web: studiofnt.com
○ Type: Saol Display, Capture Display and Noh Optique Display.

'Not Really Now Not Anymore' is the debut solo album by Nuck, an established South Korean hip-hop artist. This album serves as a musical narrative that reflects his journey concerning his mother's illness. The experience of a family member's illness or death is a profound trauma that affects both the individual and the entire family. However, it is also a journey of overcoming and reconciliation, forming this record's core theme. To capture the album's mood, Studio fnt selected a drawing from Freydal, an unfinished illustrated prose epic created during the Holy Roman Empire, for the cover. The chosen illustration portrays a moment of intense collision between two competitors in a jousting tournament. Studio fnt juxtaposed it with crushing and crumbling letters to enhance the emotional impact further. This artistic choice symbolises the intense struggle and challenges faced in life, resonating with the themes explored in the album. ●

'Abmo deliberately mixed various typefaces, papers, colours, and textures to evoke the feeling of entering a beloved personal space.'

BUCI

○ Design: Abmo
○ Web: abmo.fr
○ Type: Logo—Custom. Other—Neuf, Instrument Serif, Windsor Elongated, Ehmke Antique and Imperial Script.

The Buci is a boutique hotel nestled in the heart of the vibrant Saint Germain neighbourhood of Paris, offering a unique blend of homey intimacy and eclectic design.

Abmo deliberately mixed various typefaces, papers, colours, and textures to evoke the feeling of entering a beloved personal space, stepping away from traditional, predictable branding to mirror the distinct comfort of a home rich with stories.

Abmo's brand essence extends into a subtle layer of sensuality throughout the hotel's branding and physical space, from inviting materials to an interior design that plays with light and shadow, alongside curated art that stirs emotions and connections. This approach goes beyond aesthetics, creating an environment that invites guests to immerse themselves deeply into their senses. ●

'Abmo's brand essence extends into a subtle layer of sensuality throughout the hotel's branding and physical space, from inviting materials to an interior design that plays with light and shadow, alongside curated art that stirs emotions and connections.'

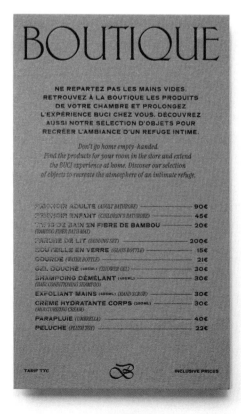

LA NUIT EST COMME UN SANCTUAIRE ELLE PORTE À L'INTIMITÉ

BUCI

Penser est une affaire intime

— GILBERT DURAND —

REFUGE INTIME

AU BUCI ON SE RETROUVE. SOI-MÊME,
À DEUX OU AVEC SES PROCHES
DANS LE CALME CHAUD DE NOTRE HÔTEL.

RÉFUGIEZ-VOUS DANS LE CONFORT
DU LIEU, ET PROFITEZ
DE VOTRE INTIMITÉ RETROUVÉE.

RESSOURCEZ-VOUS, PARTAGEZ
UNE PAUSE, AVANT DE RETOURNER
À PARIS ET AU MONDE.

— GILBERT DURAND —

« Lait et miel sont douceur, délices de l'intimité retrouvée. »

Felfel Festival

○ Design: Brest Brest Brest
○ Web: brestbrestbrest.fr
○ Type: Primary—Gaya. Other—Plaak.

The Fondation Cartier pour l'art contemporain and the Institut du monde arabe joined forces to present the first edition of Felfel, a festival of North African cultures in France. The visual identity was conceived by Brest Brest Brest, printed with two Pantone colours (warm red + violet), and using Gaya (© Raphaël de La Morinerie/Out of the Dark) as the main typeface. The font Plaak (© 205TF) is also used to support Gaya. ●

PREMIÈRE ÉDITION

2028

felfel

FESTIVAL DE L'EFFERVESCENCE DES CULTURES MAGHRÉBINES EN FRANCE

12·13·14 JUILLET
FONDATION CARTIER POUR L'ART CONTEMPORAIN & INSTITUT DU MONDE ARABE

PROJECTIONS KARAOKÉ CONCERTS BAL

DIRECTION ARTISTIQUE NAÏMA HUBER-YAHI

création ©© Brest Brest Brest

FondationCartier
pour l'art contemporain

PROGRAMMATION & RÉSERVATIONS
FONDATIONCARTIER.COM   IMARABE.ORG

INSTITUT DU MONDE ARABE

Skip the glass & pour directly into your mouth.

Kork

Wine made easy.

Kork

○ Design: Foundry
○ Web: studiofoundry.co.uk
○ Type: Temeraire Italienne Italic (modified)
   and Aeonik Regular.

Grapes are simple, and Kork believe drinking them should be too.

Kork are re-thinking how we enjoy wine by serving the good stuff in a can. It's wine made easy —but also wine to save the planet.

Compared to traditional glass wine bottles, Kork's aluminium cans use much less energy, water and oxygen in their production. They're also lighter too, so leave a much smaller transport footprint.

Foundry created a look which connects to the modern wine lover and leaves the snobbery behind. A beautifully simple product with endless benefits, emphasised by an expressive brand with an honest voice to revolutionise the world of wine. ●

Bianco
Chardonnay

A wonder... ...h a delicate and
impecca... ...fresh, juicy and
notes, w... ...es of cherry,
Lemony... ...wberry intertwine
...f black fruit.

3 units • Vegan • 200ml

Allergy Advice: Contains Sulphites

Produced and bottled by: Viña Cor...
Sur S.A., Nueva Tajamar 481, Torre
Norte, OF. 1901, Santiago, Chile.

Ha...
Or...

Chile...

Ha Bianco
Chardonnay

An earthy wine with a delicate and bright red colour, fresh, juicy and crisp red-fruit notes of cherry, raspberry and strawberry intertwine with softer traces of black fruit.

3 uni Vegan • 200ml

Allerg Contains Sulphites

Produ led by: Viña Cono Sur S.A amar 481, Torre Nora f antiago, Chile.

879452 335672

○ Daniel Peter
○ Ingrid Picanyol
Studio
○ Brest Brest Brest
○ Thought & Found
○ Studio Furious

Condensed type

Swiss Alpine Museum

○ Design: Daniel Peter ○ Web: herrpeter.ch ○ Type: Druk.

The Swiss Alpine Museum shows thematic exhibitions on the Alpine region. Changes caused by climate change, spatial development and tourism are brought to life in participatory projects. The exhibition 'Heimat. Tracing the Story of Mitholz' is a project with people from a Swiss mountain village about memory, risk and responsibility. After the Second World War, there was a catastrophic explosion in an ammunition depot, which destroyed most of the houses and killed nine people. The residents will have to leave their homes for 10 years due to clearance work at the ammunition depot in 2030. Daniel Peter conceptualised and designed the communication, exhibition graphics and the publication. ●

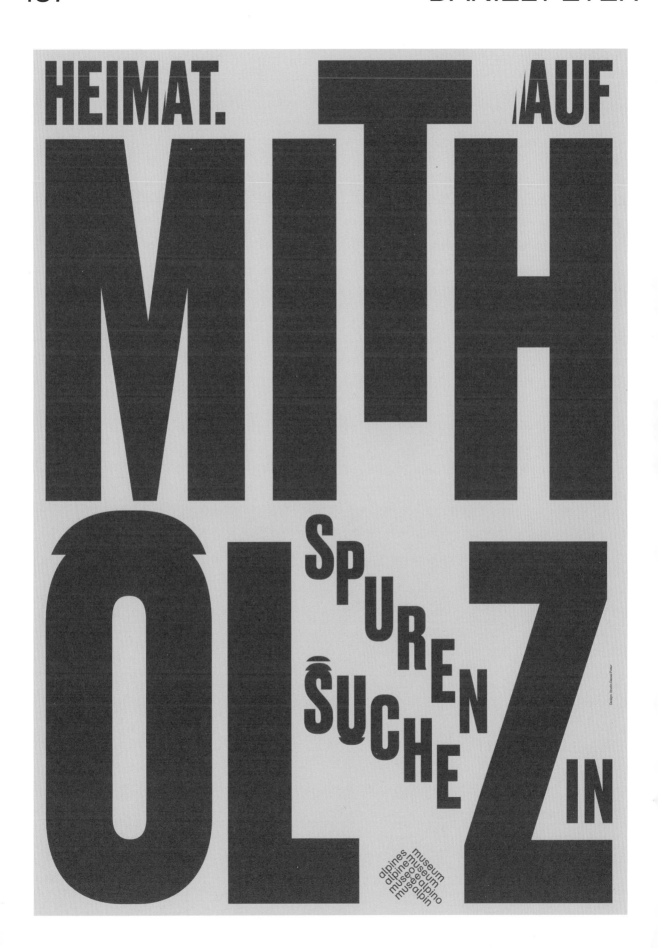

Ingrid Picanyol

HOW DID YOU BECOME INVOLVED IN GRAPHIC DESIGN?

I fell in love with this discipline on the last day of my photography degree. They proposed to us, as an exercise, to design our own business cards, so we could begin officially as photographers, and there I discovered how much fun I had thinking about how I could present myself on a small piece of paper no larger than 85x55mm.

Although, if I look back, I realise that I already had contact with the discipline before, because from the ages of sixteen to nineteen I designed flyers for the concerts we did with my punk band, using Corel Draw. And, if I look back further, I see myself trying to imitate the graffiti letters that my brother and other boys made on the walls of the town where I grew up and on the trains that took us to see the city.

So, instead of becoming a photographer, I decided to start studying graphic design and continue working in the hospitality industry. I saw that exercise of designing our own business cards as a vocational sign, but also as a job with which I could earn my living, without having to spend a fortune—which I didn't have—on cameras, lenses and flashes. I left my parent's house when I was only sixteen years old, so my own finances have influenced many of the decisions I have made throughout my life.

The place where I consider that I really forged the foundations on which I have built myself as designer was at Suki Design Studio, located in the city of Vic. I started working there without having finished my studies and in that kitchen full of Macs and paper catalogues, Marcel Lladó and Quim Marin dedicated themselves with patience and enthusiasm to shaping my way of seeing, feeding my mental library of references, and cementing my relationship between typography and grids, and between positive and negative space. ○

CAN YOU SHARE YOUR PROCESS FOR DEVELOPING CONCEPTS AND SKETCHES WHEN STARTING A NEW PROJECT FOCUSED ON EXPRESSIVE TYPOGRAPHY? HOW DO YOU REFINE YOUR IDEAS TO ENSURE THEY EFFECTIVELY COMMUNICATE THE INTENDED MESSAGE OR EMOTION?

When I start working on a project, I always write. I try to describe the project in many different ways. I summarise it in multiple ways to reach different conclusions and to find similarities between the assignment and other things that could have some kind of metaphorical relationship. So, from the beginning, one of the things that I explore the most is the story. After that story, I start to work on the form, exploring resources that can help me convey it visually.

I ask myself a lot of questions about how I can convey the idea, without having to explain it, so that it is easily recognised by the viewer. I have the final audience of the project in mind, even more so than my client, because they are the one I want to establish a relationship with. It's with them that I wish to communicate.

I wish to invite the audience to connect the ends of the conceptual threads of the proposal, because, when that happens, the experience is unforgettable for the end user. So when I design, I always have the client in mind but also the end user, and even my mother. On the one hand, I fantasize about expanding the horizon of our practice by contributing something new. On the other hand, I wish a broader audience would understand our work. And with that I'm not saying that my mother is a better or worse image reader, I simply take her into account because she is a distant person of the profession that also has to be able to read and understand it. ○

CAN YOU SHARE A PROJECT WHERE YOU USED TYPOGRAPHY AS A PRIMARY MEANS OF EXPRESSION? WHAT MESSAGE OR EMOTION WERE YOU TRYING TO CONVEY, AND HOW DID YOU ACHIEVE IT THROUGH TYPOGRAPHY?

————————————

The design of the identity of the Masvell restaurant is an example of a project focused on typography. It is an emblematic space for the town of Masnou, which is located inside a modernist building from the beginning of the century. The place is loaded with so much history that both the architect Stefano Colli and I were very careful that every design decision we took would respect the place itself. We both set ourselves the condition of trying to rescue elements that had already been there previously, or could have been there, before deciding to incorporate new features. Therefore, when beginning to develop the identity visually, I wondered if any typeface had inhabited the place throughout its history.

Every identity needs a font to be able to communicate, so I investigated if I could find one in the interiors of the space, on the facades or in historical documents.

I wanted to find a group of characters from which I could design an alphabet, and with it, develop the identity of a place as authentic and unique as Masvell. During that process, I discovered the original hand-drawn plans of the building that the architect Bonaventura Bassegoda had designed a century earlier. So I decided to call typographer Noe Blanco to help me design a typeface based on the characteristics of Bassegoda's handwritten calligraphy at the time of designing the building. With that alphabet as the main ingredient, we create an identity that does not need to contain a logo on each application, because any word or text used carries Masvell's own voice integrated within it. ○

————————————
————————————

HOW DO YOU APPROACH THE PROCESS OF SELECTING TYPEFACES FOR PROJECTS THAT REQUIRE A STRONG EMOTIONAL OR EXPRESSIVE IMPACT? WHAT FACTORS DO YOU CONSIDER?

————————————

Within my projects there is always a single concept that acts as a lighthouse and guides all the decisions I make. That concept is the most important thing within my work, and any resource that does not work in its favour I consider inappropriate and unnecessary.

One of the main factors that I take into account in those projects where the selection and use of typography is the best choice to translate the concept of the identity, is to avoid choosing a font that is in fashion. I find it incoherent to see several projects coexisting at the same time that use the same source. I feel that the typography is the voice of the project, so it seems strange to me that the same voice is used in different projects. I also take other factors into account. For example, I consider the moment in which a typeface was designed and how that can influence its relevance and appropriateness for a specific project. ○

————————————
————————————

EXPRESSIVE TYPOGRAPHY OFTEN INVOLVES BREAKING TRADITIONAL TYPOGRAPHIC RULES. HOW DO YOU STRIKE A BALANCE BETWEEN BREAKING CONVENTIONS AND ENSURING CLARITY AND EFFECTIVENESS IN COMMUNICATION?

————————————

I try to achieve this by collaborating with and trusting people who are specialists within that field. When I have collaborated with the typographer Noe Blanco, I have come to the conclusion that she has an eye more tuned than mine to appreciate if we are going in a direction that is too expressive or if, otherwise, we can exaggerate it a little more. Something that I always take note of, is that it is essential that this exercise is carried out taking into account the size at which typography will be used, since it is this that determines the risk of loss of legibility. ○

————————————
————————————

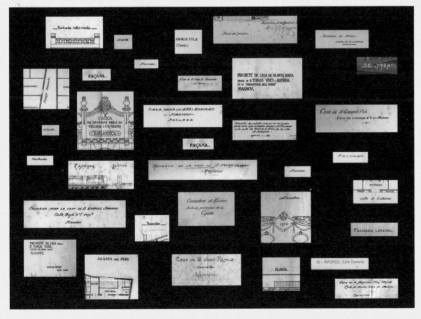

◁ Masvell, typographic inspiration.

HOW DO YOU STAY INSPIRED AND CONTINUOUSLY PUSH THE BOUNDARIES IN YOUR DESIGN WORK? ARE THERE ANY SPECIFIC ARTISTS, MOVEMENTS, OR DESIGN TECHNIQUES THAT INFLUENCE YOUR CREATIVE PROCESS?

One of the things that inspires me the most is the possibility of pushing the boundaries of the profession. I seek to resolve assignments in a sincere and consistent manner with an honesty toward the project, but I also try to contribute something new to the design sector. I firmly believe that projects can be approached in various ways, and that objectivity is difficult to achieve due to human influence in regards to decisions about what is appropriate and what is not, for example.

Therefore, when faced with various possibilities, I am always enthusiastic about the one that risks the most and contains the potential for innovation in the sector, thus expanding the possibilities of our profession.

To achieve this, I surround myself with books of literature and poetry, I take writing courses, I learn to play instruments, I listen to lectures by creative people from different fields outside of design, I watch movies and observe the street in search of graphic resources. I am not limited to look at design to do design, but I immerse myself in everything else, since I spent many years focused solely on design. O

HOW DO YOU MEASURE THE SUCCESS OF YOUR DESIGN WORK? CAN YOU PROVIDE EXAMPLES OF PROJECTS WHERE YOUR USE OF DESIGN HAD A SIGNIFICANT IMPACT ON THE AUDIENCE OR CLIENT OBJECTIVES?

I believe that a success story goes beyond the simple satisfaction of both the client and myself with the final result, although this aspect is fundamental. Other important factors include the project's ability to capture the attention of your target audience, as well as direct and indirect competition. Furthermore, although to a lesser extent, success can also be measured by the project's impact on the design sector, by providing innovation in an environment increasingly saturated with formality and work that is similar to one other. O

CAN YOU DISCUSS A PROJECT WHERE YOU USED UNCONVENTIONAL MATERIALS OR METHODS TO CREATE EXPRESSIVE TYPOGRAPHY?

We have recently redeveloped a highly expressive typography to strengthen a brand identity, in collaboration with typographer Noe Blanco. I started by creating an alphabet with vectors in Adobe Illustrator, combining an existing font with letters cut-out physically from paper with scissors. With this initial material, Noe was in charge of redrawing the characters, creating alternatives, and designing a family of punctuation marks. O

DO YOU HAVE A FAVOURITE FONT AND WHY?

I don't have a favourite font, since I think that all of them can be ideal for certain occasions. Even Comic Sans, despite the criticism it has received, could be suitable to communicate a specific concept. However, I must admit that when exploring projects where typography is not a prominent resource, I tend to automatically select fonts such as Monreal, Helvetica, Neue Haas or Suisse, without much reflection. O

WHAT ARE YOUR GOALS FOR THE FUTURE OF YOUR COMPANY?

Continue working on projects that I am truly passionate about, alongside clients with whom I have a good connection, and with collaborators who are not only great professionals, but also good humans. I aspire to maintain a positive and collaborative work environment, where professional excellence is combined with interpersonal relationships. ●

Wepa!

O Design: Ingrid Picanyol Studio
O Web: ingridpicanyol.com
O Type: FK Screamer and Portrait.

Wepa! Coffee sells Puerto Rican coffee. They approached Ingrid Picanyol Studio to design their graphic identity and packaging, which needed to reflect the island's spirit. The term 'Boricua', as locals call themselves, embodies pride and joy.

    The name 'Wepa!' exudes excitement, echoing Puerto Rican exuberance. Ingrid Picanyol Studio accentuated this through the use of playful typography, intentionally avoiding any clichés. The design features bold colours, inspired by traditional coffee packaging. Puerto Rico's lush rainforests inspired the packaging pattern, using repeated 'W' motifs. Ingrid Picanyol Studio's goal was to capture the essence of Puerto Rico, beyond its beaches, with rhythmic compositions and vibrant colours, their designs embody the lively spirit of Boricua culture. ●

PORTES-LÈS-VALENCE
04 75 57 14 55
TRAIN-THEATRE.FR
Licences 1-089115 2-009668 3-009569

SCÈNE CONVENTIONNÉE
D'INTÉRÊT NATIONAL
ART & CRÉATION,
CHANSON FRANCOPHONE

LE TRAIN THÉÂTRE 2022 2023

Réservations
dès le 16 juin
13h30

Billetterie
en ligne
train-theatre.fr

Le Train Théâtre

○ Design: Brest Brest Brest ○ Web: brestbrestbrest.fr ○ Type: Pimpit and Hermes.

This visual identity was made for the French concert hall Le Train Théâtre by the studio Brest Brest Brest. Each visual is conceived from a single monotone colour. The logo and identity were designed with the fonts Pimpit (© Benoît Bodhuin) and Hermes (© Optimo). ●

Poster 1 (top left)

 Le Train Théâtre

PORTES-LÈS-VALENCE
04 75 57 14 95
TRAIN-THEATRE.FR
SCÈNE CONVENTIONNÉE
D'INTÉRÊT NATIONAL
ART & CRÉATION,
CHANSON FRANCOPHONE

CIRQUE 23 24

LE TRAIN THÉÂTRE A 30 ANS !

6+7 OCT
SANS CULOTTE
CIE GALAPIAT
+ LES JOSIANES

6+7+8 DÉC
RÉVOLTE
LES FILLES DU
RENARD PÂLE

5+6+7 MAR
LA GALERIE
MACHINE
DE CIRQUE

20 MAR
BASKETTEUSES
DE BAMAKO
CIE TG

10+11+12 AVR
A SIMPLE SPACE
GRAVITY &
OTHER MYTHS

Poster 2 (top right)

Le Train Théâtre

PORTES-LÈS-VALENCE
04 75 57 14 95
TRAIN-THEATRE.FR
SCÈNE CONVENTIONNÉE
D'INTÉRÊT NATIONAL
ART & CRÉATION,
CHANSON FRANCOPHONE

DANSE 23 24

13 MAR
D'UN RÊVE
CIE MOUVEMENTS PERPÉTUELS

6 AVR
TEMPUS
CIE VOLTAÏK

Poster 3 (bottom left)

 Le Train Théâtre

PORTES-LÈS-VALENCE
04 75 57 14 95
TRAIN-THEATRE.FR
SCÈNE CONVENTIONNÉE
D'INTÉRÊT NATIONAL
ART & CRÉATION,
CHANSON FRANCOPHONE

JEUNE PUBLIC EN FAMILLE

3 NOV
SUR LES PAS
D'OODAAQ
CIE LES DÉCINTRÉS
→ LES CLÉVOS

29 NOV
(Y'A DU MONDE SUR)
LA CORDALINGE
JEREM

13 DÉC
L'AU-DESSUS
NICOLAS LOPEZ

24 JAN
CHAMBRE
CIE DU BRUIT
DANS LA TÊTE

14 FÉV
NOS PALAIS INTIMES
RÊVE D'AIR
RÊVE DE PIERRE
CIE LA TORTUE

27 MAR
AH ! LES VOYAGES
CIE EN FORME

3 AVR
EN APPARENCE
TONY MELVIL
& MARIE LEVAVASSEUR

19 AVR
ANATOPIES
JUSTINE MACADOUX
& J-A DUPONT
CASTRO
→ LES CLÉVOS

29 MAI
LA BERGÈRE AUX
MAINS BLEUES
AMÉLIE-LES-CRAYONS

Poster 4 (bottom right)

Le Train Théâtre

PORTES-LÈS-VALENCE
04 75 57 14 95
TRAIN-THEATRE.FR
SCÈNE CONVENTIONNÉE
D'INTÉRÊT NATIONAL
ART & CRÉATION,
CHANSON FRANCOPHONE

TIM DUP

jeu 19 octobre 20h   chanson

première partie   ARTHUR ELY

    **train-theatre.fr**

Mamma Chen's

○ Design: Thought & Found ○ Web: thoughtandfound.co ○ Type: Logo—Custom.
Other—Mandrel, Acumin, Prestige Elite, Aria and Hiragino Kaku Gothic.

Mamma Chen's is a live music venue dedicated to championing equity—providing warm, safe spaces for artists to share, engage and perform in. The visual identity uses an eclectic range of logotypes, typefaces and illustrations to celebrate diversity in multiple aspects; the patrons, the artists and their voices, and the cultural richness of the location. The flexibility represented in the execution highlights the venue's adaptability and nurturing atmosphere, encouraging creativity on all fronts; emphasising and supporting the venue's founding ambition. A contrasting colour palette is used throughout to celebrate the engaging and energetic atmosphere of Mamma Chen's. ●

Rūlo

○ Design: Studio Furious
○ Web: studiofurious.com
○ Type: Hiragino Kaku Gothic.

Rūlo is a sushi handroll spot in Paris, France, located on rue Saint-Maur. The brand identity was designed by Quentin Weisbuch (Studio Furious), using Obviously by OH no Type Co. in wide and compressed versions.

The typeface, with its sharp angles, contrasts with the round shapes that are used all around the shop: the spinning menu and shop sign, the stools and even the wallpaper with its wavy effect that refers to the sushi roll. For the Japanese text, Studio Furious worked with a bold weight from Hiragino Kaku Gothic. ●

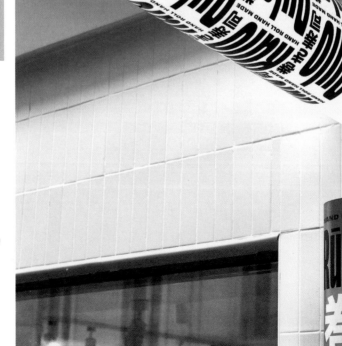

'The typeface, with its sharp angles, contrasts with the round shapes that are used all around the shop.'

○ Atelier Avocado
○ Studio fnt
○ Fons Hickmann
   M23
○ DE_FORM

3D
type

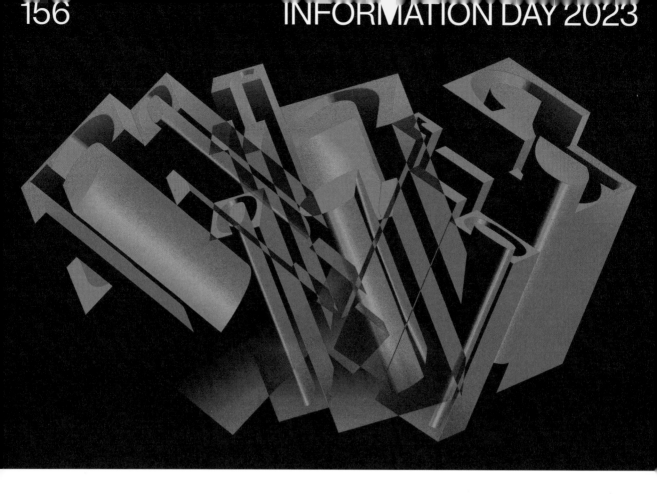

Information Day 2023 | HKU Architecture

○ Design: Atelier Avocado
○ Web: atelieravocado.com
○ Type: Trade Gothic Next.

Information Day is an annual event of the University of Hong Kong, welcoming prospective students, staff and mentors to gather and share academic experiences through admission talks, workshops and campus tours. The key visual is created from the extrusions and dissections of the faculty acronym FOA. The animated 3D forms were transformed into a set of visuals with different angles and colouration dedicated to the five bachelor degree courses of the faculty. The multi-faceted identity accentuates the diversity and versatility of the faculty education spectrum. ●

BA(LS)

Bachelor of Arts in
Landscape Studies

BASc(Design+)

Bachelor of Arts and
Sciences in Design+

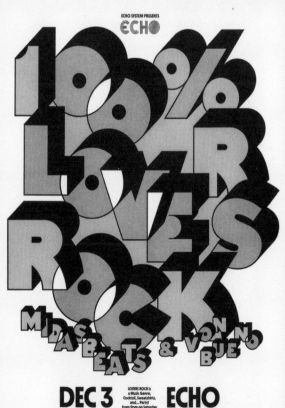

100% LOVERS ROCK

○ Design: Studio fnt
○ Web: studiofnt.com
○ Type: P22 Glaser Kitchen Regular
 and MD Nichrome 0.8.

100% LOVERS ROCK is a DJing event by Melody Bar Echo in Seoul. Originally, Lovers' Rock was a style of reggae music that added a soft sound and sensibility to its baseline and rhythm. This genre consists of many romantic songs. Lovers' Rock is also the name of a cocktail, as well as the name of the sweatshirts they sell and the title of this party, as indicated on the poster. Studio fnt portrayed this romantic, end-of-year, seasonal event using round, thick letters that embrace and harmonise with each other. ●

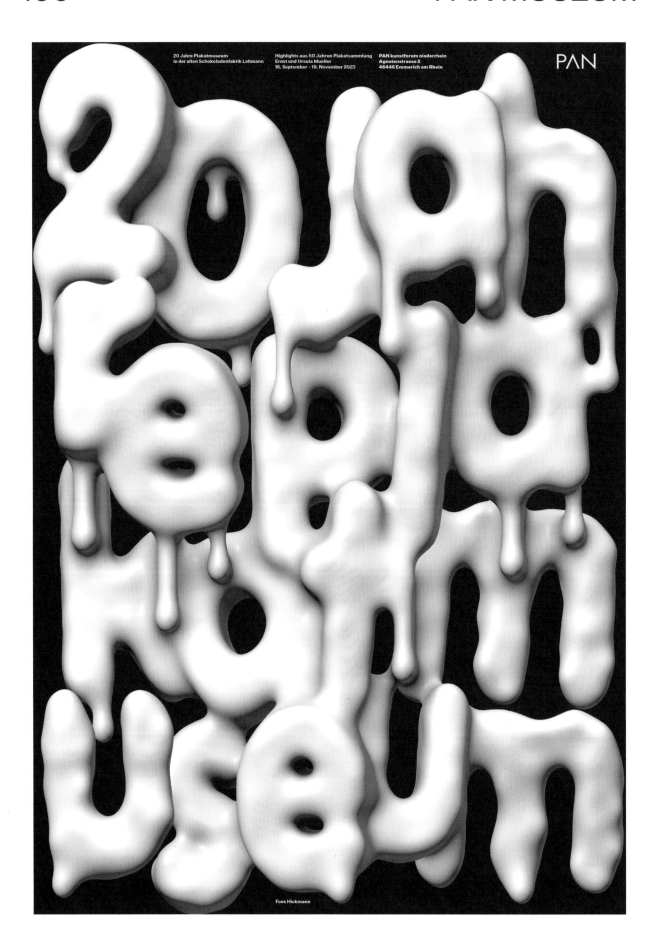

20 Jahre Plakatmuseum
in der alten Schokoladenfabrik Lohmann

Highlights aus 50 Jahren Plakatsammlung
Ernst und Ursula Mueller
16. September – 19. November 2023

PAN kunstforum niederrhein
Agnetenstrasse 2
46446 Emmerich am Rhein

PAN

Fons Hickmann

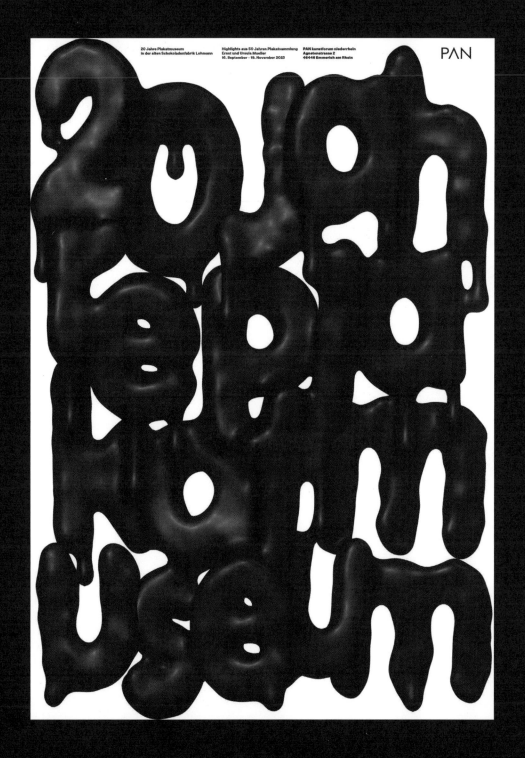

PAN Museum

O Design: Fons Hickmann M23 O Web: fonshickmann.com O Type: Custom.

This diptych of posters celebrates the anniversary of the PAN Museum in Emmerich.
The words, '20 Years of Poster Museum', are creatively fused in a tongue-in-cheek manner
with chocolate analogies, paying homage to the museum's unique location in a repurposed,
old chocolate factory. These two posters reference each other, as they promote two
different events, prompting the question, 'do you prefer white or dark chocolate?' ●

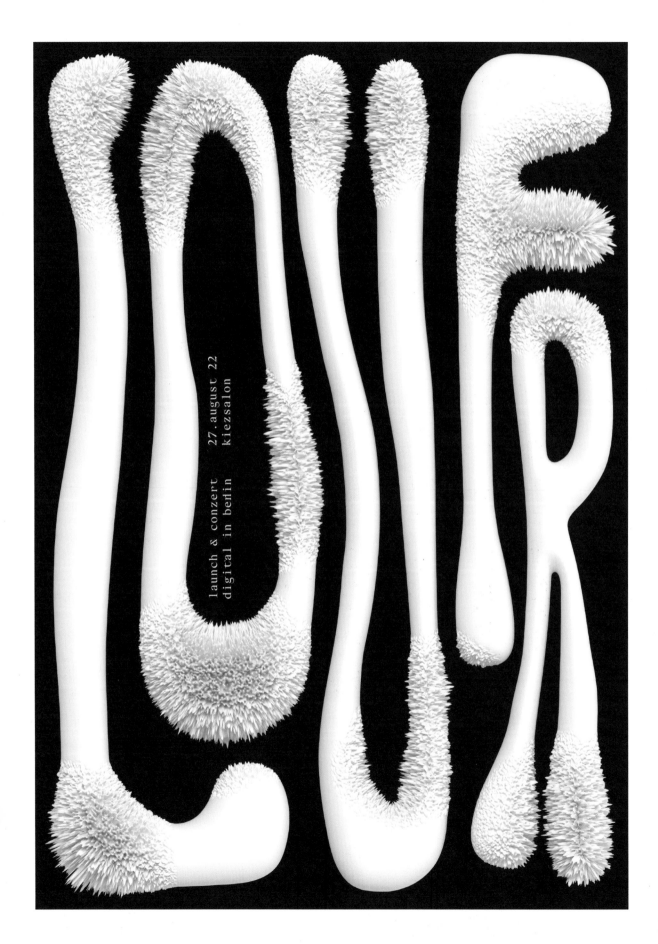

launch & conzert   27. august 22
digital in berlin   kiezsalon

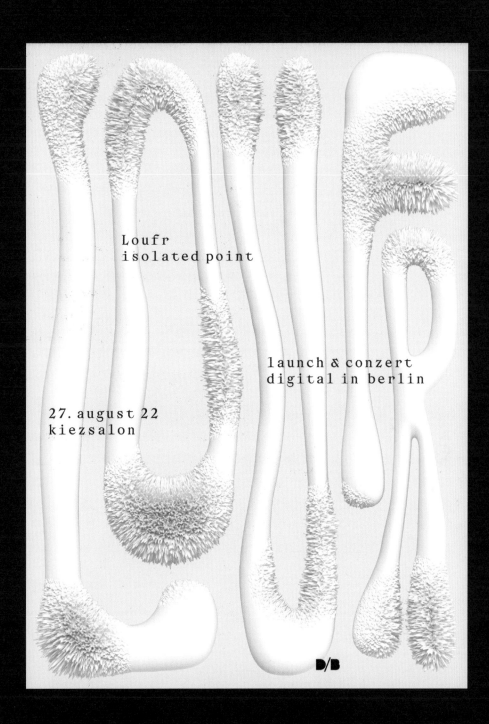

Loufr
isolated point

launch & conzert
digital in berlin

27. august 22
kiezsalon

D/B

LOUFR

○ Design: Fons Hickmann M23 ○ Web: fonshickmann.com ○ Type: Custom.

The album 'Isolated Point' by LOUFR draws on elements from club music, IDM, as well as vocal manipulation. Behind LOUFR is Polish composer Piotr Bednarczyk, who lives and works as a musician and physician in Warsaw. His sound collages focus mainly on instrumental electroacoustic and electronic music. Fons Hickmann M23 designed a biometric 'LOUFR' lettering. The materiality of their key visual is not intended to be assignable and to sit somewhere between a synthetic material and a natural product. A kind of biological growth of a non-biological species ●

'The project's hallmark is
an interactive visual system
designed to digitally reimagine
physical exhibitions, offering
a novel experience beyond
traditional attendance.'

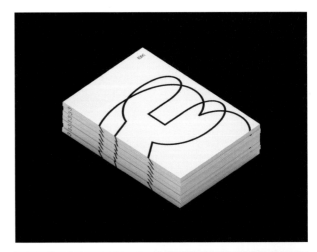

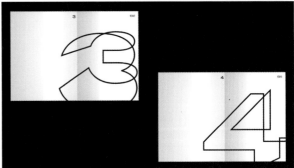

DE_FORM

Beyond Matter

○ Design: DE_FORM
○ Web: de-form.hu
○ Type: Söhne Breit.

BEYOND MATTER is a dynamic, international initiative aimed at revitalising landmark exhibitions from the past and showcasing current ones through both physical and digital mediums, organised by ZKM Karlsruhe.

The project's hallmark is an interactive visual system designed to digitally reimagine physical exhibitions, offering a novel experience beyond traditional attendance. DE_FORM represented this dynamic digital space using simple graphic tools. They created an optical effect that effectively reflects the relationship between the digital and the physical space. ●

○ Paz Miamor
○ Sitoh
○ Brand Brothers
○ Thought & Found
○ CENTER
○ Seachange
○ About Contact
○ Universal Favourite
○ Studio Tempo
○ Super Studio

Custom type

Tallo

O Design: Paz Miamor O Web: pazmiamor.com O Type: Logo—Custom. Other—Nimbus Sans Regular.

Tallo is a local brand of cold-pressed juices produced in Buenos Aires, Argentina. The graphic idea represents a flower or a fruit instead of the stem itself (Tallo), which brings a natural feel to the brand. The colours of these juices are both vibrant and pastel at the same time. The colour palette of the labels vibrates with the colour of the juice, to create a fun atmosphere. In addition to a bold geometric logo, the design contains small linear illustrations to represent the ingredients. This is a reference to the drawings of the brand creators' daughters. ●

för ägg

○ Design: Sitoh
○ Web: sitoh.co.jp
○ Type: Logo—Custom. Other—Calluna.

This rebranding and design work was created by Sitoh for 'för ägg', a Japanese confectionery company and shop. The rebrand references the change and development from eggs to cake.

Sitoh created a logotype and logo mark using the grid to reresent a cracked egg. A raw egg is then represented by the double circle, and a chiffon cake is conveyed by the changing of this egg. Typography is created within the constraints of the grid, as is the form of a chicken. ●

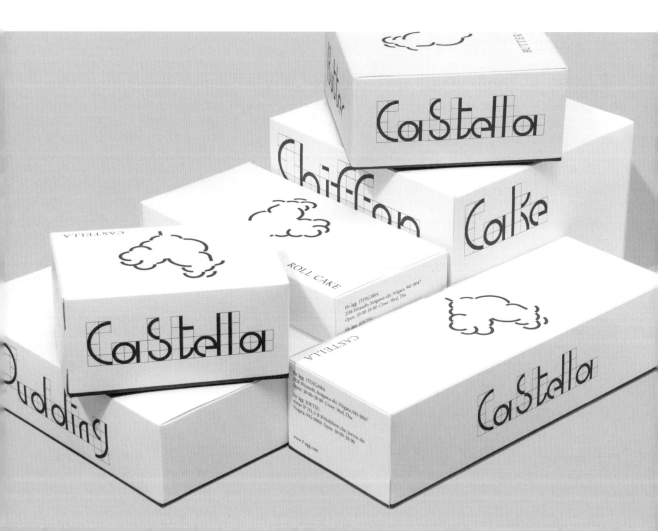

för ägg ITOIGAWA
2116 Hiraishi, Itoigawa-shi, Niigata, 941-0047
Open: 10:00–18:00 Close: Wed, Thu

för ägg JOETSU
1F 113-3-8-8 Nishihon-cho, Joetsu-shi, Niigata, 942-0004

'The proposal is based on a typogram with a logical, organised structure, but punctuated by graphic accidents that give it a character that is both charismatic and welcoming.'

Studio Hauteville

O Design: Brand Brothers
O Web: brandbrothers.studio
O Type: Logo—Custom. Other—Aspekta 400.

Studio Hauteville is a photo and video studio located at 3 rue d'Hauteville, in the heart of Paris. The 160m² studio offers photographers, creative directors and producers a full range of high-end services in an intimate atmosphere. Brand Brothers was commissioned to design the visual identity for the inauguration of the venue in spring 2023.

    The proposal is based on a typogram with a logical, organised structure, but punctuated by graphic accidents that give it a character that is both charismatic and welcoming. This identity is brought to life on multiple media, including a series of graphic posters that enhance the studio's interior design. ●

STUDIO HAUTEVILLE

3 RUE D'HAUTEVILLE   75010 PARIS
TEL   0033 6 02 49 40 36
INFO   (AT)   STUDIOHAUTEVILLE.COM
INSTAGRAM (AT) STUDIOHAUTEVILLE
WEB   STUDIOHAUTEVILLE.COM

3 RUE D'HAUTEVILLE   75010 PARIS
TEL   0033 6 02 49 40 36
INFO   (AT)   STUDIOHAUTEVILLE.COM
INSTAGRAM (AT) STUDIOHAUTEVILLE
WEB   STUDIOHAUTEVILLE.COM

Amery Oke-Johnston

HOW DID YOU BECOME INVOLVED IN GRAPHIC DESIGN?

It's always so interesting to try and pinpoint that exact moment (outside of the academic setting). Like a lot of people who have pursued a journey into design, I was always interested in some sort of creative occupation—as a youth, I often oscillated between wanting to be an artist or designer. It probably wasn't until endeavouring into further education that I decided to pursue graphic design, seeing there was the capacity to integrate my more artistic and expressive sensibilities into design executions. ⟲

CAN YOU SHARE YOUR PROCESS FOR DEVELOPING CONCEPTS AND SKETCHES WHEN STARTING A NEW PROJECT FOCUSED ON EXPRESSIVE TYPOGRAPHY? HOW DO YOU REFINE YOUR IDEAS TO ENSURE THEY EFFECTIVELY COMMUNICATE THE INTENDED MESSAGE OR EMOTION?

Prior to commencing any creative executions, the process begins with unpacking the underlying values (or narrative) of a project. Unearthing the core values and positioning of a brand or project starts to illustrate the possible atmospheric qualities and avenues that might be sought during concept development—e.g. Is it a gentle, bold, or dynamic voice? It's these initial defining qualities that begin to translate messages and emotions into visual outcomes. ⟲

CAN YOU SHARE A PROJECT WHERE YOU USED TYPOGRAPHY AS A PRIMARY MEANS OF EXPRESSION? WHAT MESSAGE OR EMOTION WERE YOU TRYING TO CONVEY, AND HOW DID YOU ACHIEVE IT THROUGH TYPOGRAPHY?

Mamma Chen's is definitely a key project that uses typography as a means of conveying both impact and emotive sentiments. Mamma Chen's, for context, is a live music venue in Naarm/Melbourne dedicated to boldly championing equity. The agreed narrative, of celebrating diversity, led to an approach that embodied an energetic eclecticism. A series of logotypes were developed, ranging from the depiction of traditional to non-traditional forms; the broad array of typographic silhouettes illustrated the idea of unique voices, artists, and patrons. The breadth of flexibility in the branded execution and supporting typographic arrangements highlights the venue's adaptability and nurturing atmosphere to encourage creativity, emphasizing and supporting the venue's founding ambition. ⟲

△ Mamma Chen's.

HOW DO YOU APPROACH THE PROCESS OF SELECTING TYPEFACES FOR PROJECTS THAT REQUIRE A STRONG EMOTIONAL OR EXPRESSIVE IMPACT? WHAT FACTORS DO YOU CONSIDER?

The selection process is informed by initially determining the type of voice held (by a brand or project). The clarity offered from these messages or determinations can help guide the decision-making process and formulate options that speak true to emotive qualities or expressive narratives. ⟲

EXPRESSIVE TYPOGRAPHY OFTEN INVOLVES BREAKING TRADITIONAL TYPOGRAPHIC RULES. HOW DO YOU STRIKE A BALANCE BETWEEN BREAKING CONVENTIONS AND ENSURING CLARITY AND EFFECTIVENESS IN COMMUNICATION?

By breaking convention, I think we strike a new idea of 'balance', 'clarity' and 'effectiveness'. As a whole, these qualifiers are subjective, and some might even note expressive typography to be unclear. The beauty in impactful and emotive strains of typography is that in its execution, its pure purpose is to emote and align to a much larger narrative. 'Balance', 'clarity' and 'effectiveness' is then instead read through the lens of connecting and feeling. ○

HOW DO YOU STAY INSPIRED AND CONTINUOUSLY PUSH THE BOUNDARIES IN YOUR DESIGN WORK? ARE THERE ANY SPECIFIC ARTISTS, MOVEMENTS, OR DESIGN TECHNIQUES THAT INFLUENCE YOUR CREATIVE PROCESS?

I honestly like to take a healthy dose of not being creative at all in my free time! I think it's important to give ourselves the space to recharge and reconnect with the world, ourselves, and the people that surround us. ○

HOW DO YOU MEASURE THE SUCCESS OF YOUR DESIGN WORK? CAN YOU PROVIDE EXAMPLES OF PROJECTS WHERE YOUR USE OF DESIGN HAD A SIGNIFICANT IMPACT ON THE AUDIENCE OR CLIENT OBJECTIVES?

My process is generally rooted in feeling, which lends itself to generating ideas that capture emotional sentiments through non-conventional expressions—it's about using that chemistry to create something meaningful. So, for me, success can only be measured through alignment, where we see both the audience and client relate to visual outcomes—capturing the idea of feeling 'seen'. ○

CAN YOU DISCUSS A PROJECT WHERE YOU USED UNCONVENTIONAL MATERIALS OR METHODS TO CREATE EXPRESSIVE TYPOGRAPHY?

My starting point is usually some sort of rigid grid, so the foundational structure is typically very 'conventional'. With some projects it's playing within the constraints of limited frameworks to develop expressive intricacies, and in other moments, it's about exploring forms that don't conventionally fit within rigid structures or systems. ○

DO YOU HAVE A FAVOURITE FONT AND WHY?

I think an all-time favorite is Neue Haas Grotesk, which is somewhat the antithesis of what's being explored here. There's something about the lack of decorative ornamentation that feels so satisfying to look at. There's something about the family being the foundation for our initial understanding of typography that feels particularly nostalgic. It's a relatable beginning for many of us, leading us to further explorations about typography and its expressions. I think there are a lot of people who either love it or hate it, and there's something about that which feels very in line with expressive typography. ○

WHAT ARE YOUR GOALS FOR THE FUTURE OF YOUR COMPANY?

The desire to be seen is the desire to exist. This expression is central to both the future and present aspirations of Thought & Found. As a QTPOC designer, inclusivity and diversity play a pivotal role in my practice. The studio's objective is to continue supporting marginalized communities and individuals, delivering projects with impactful narratives that align vision and voice. An integral future aspiration of the company would be to one day expand to showcase other creatives with similar lived experiences – shining a spotlight on the importance of diversity and visibility. ●

'The beauty in impactful and emotive strains of typography is that in its execution, its pure purpose is to emote and align to a much larger narrative.'

OKE

○ Design: Thought & Found
○ Web: thoughtandfound.co
○ Type: Logo—Custom. Other—Neue Haas
   Grotesk Text Pro and IBM Plex Mono.

OKE is an interplay of shape and colour.
The identity drew influence from the business'
belief that art and design can bring life to the
spaces we inhabit and plays a vital role in
reflecting our own wonderful idiosyncrasies.
The logotype represents the playful and joyful
nature of OKE and is seen in combination with
an eclectic palette that celebrates the diversity
of the creatives' influences. ●

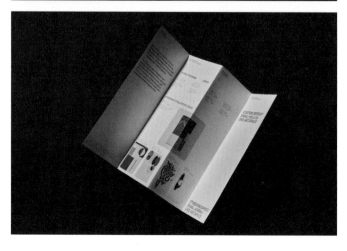

Chassie

O Design: CENTER
O Web: center.design
O Type: Chassie Display (custom) and La Nord.

Chassie, a family-run furniture business from the Bronx, had a vision to make unique desks for a world where at-home offices are the new normal. CENTER built a brand system that reflects Chassie's craftsmanship, highlighting the customisability of the products. Chassie Display, a bespoke typeface developed for the brand, was inspired by a CNC machine's router fixture plate—a Chassie studio staple. The team loved how it visually connected to the geometric 4x4 grid experiments found within Armin Hofmann's 1965 'Graphic Design Manual', and used this same grid to create custom patterns and typography as modular as the furniture Chassie produces. ●

MEET ANDREW

Since our founding in 2006, Andrew has been [he]lm (literally) of our CNC machine, the [cor]e of all Chassie products.

EARDROP [TA]BLE

CHASSIE x CUSTOM

chassie Our newest pattern drop is very special to us because it's one of the last comissions of our friend and mentor @miltonglaser.

NEWS

CHASSIE × MILTON GLASER

chassie Our newest pattern drop is very special to us because it's one of the last comissions of our friend and mentor @miltonglaser.

BUILD

SALE SALE SALE

chassie Show Mother Earth (and your wallet) some love by shopping our Showroom Sample Sale. Make your workspace work for you.

LIVE

OPEN STUDIO

MARCH 14
4–6 PM
◯ IG LIVE

 HIGH [QUALITY] SHIPS NOW BUILT FOR YOU

chassie Introducing... the *NEW* Chassie. We're saying hello again, but that doesn't mean we've changed. We're still giving you the best in quality.

SEMINAR 002

THE FUTURE OF MAKING

SEPT 12
6 PM EST
◯ IG LIVE

chassie Join us on September 12 for a conversation with artist and designer John Sohn about side projec[ts] that become main projects. #madeforyourlifeswork

 chassie

FRIENDS OF

Loot

○ Design: Seachange
○ Web: seachange.studio
○ Type: Custom.

Loot Coffee, formerly Community Coffee Co, sought a rebrand to stand out in the competitive market of Perth, Western Australia. Inspired by the region's hot, arid landscape, Seachange created a bold, fun, and memorable brand leveraging Western themes. The meticulously crafted wordmark implies value and is adaptable across various applications. Campaigns like 'Fresh Bounty' and 'Most Wanted' link the name to the product. Packaging features compostable bags with silver labels showcasing coffee characteristics and roasting dates. Western motifs like bullet holes add playful charm. Baristas are dubbed 'Espresso Outlaws', and high-fashion cowgirls and cowboys feature in brand imagery. Wanted-style posters announced the exciting launch. ●

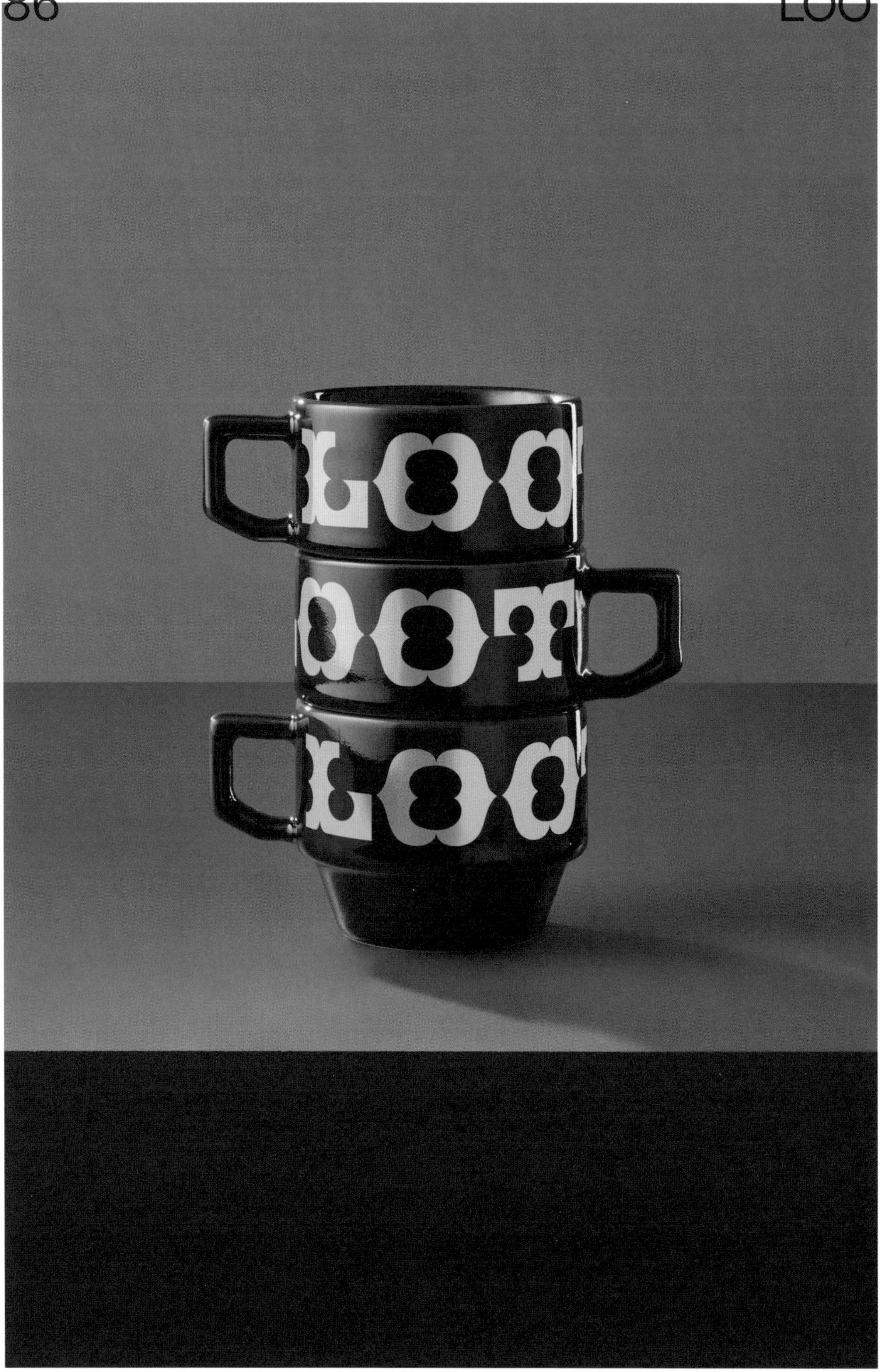
LOOT
LOOT
LOOT

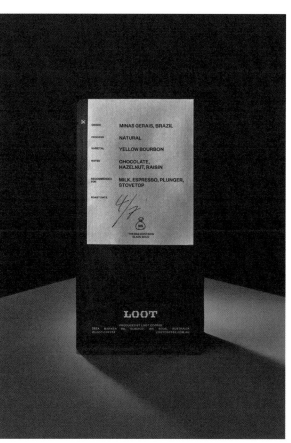

'The transitioning logo, from starry to spiky, embodies their bold 'no-nonsense' attitude, infused with an unmistakable feminine touch'.

Plenty

O Design: About Contact
O Web: aboutcontact.com
O Type: Times Now Semi-light and ABC Diatype Edu Regular.

The dynamic rebranding of 'Plenty' reflects its visionary team. Established in 2015, this collective of young entrepreneurial women has captivated both creatives and audiences with their pioneering spirit. Emerging from Antwerp's creative scene, they seamlessly integrated disciplines like music, dance, and art, resonating with their unique vision. Seeking a new identity for their podcast, 'Plenty to Say', the concept of Plenty was born. Every aspect of this branding was meticulously crafted, culminating in an animated logo created through Cavalry. The transitioning logo, from starry to spiky, embodies their bold 'no-nonsense' attitude, infused with an unmistakable feminine touch. ●

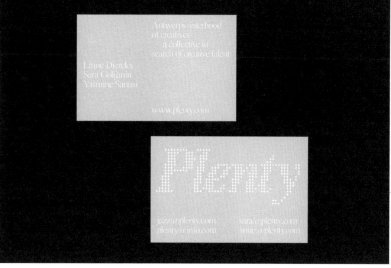

Colour Mill

○ Design: Universal Favourite
○ Web: universalfavourite.com.au
○ Type: Logo—Custom.
   Other—Studio Pro.

Colour Mill is an Australia-based food colouring brand that's been making mess in the kitchen for more than 30 years. In a category filled with subpar products, they pride themselves on their specialty pigments, which achieve unmatched creative results for their incredibly dedicated, cake-making and baking customers.

Their community is vivid and vibrant, dedicated to delightful creations, rich in colour and joy, and yet the majority of the brands providing their colouring products are dull and uninspiring. To set themselves apart, they needed an identity that would express what they've got to offer—premium, playful and kaleidoscopic colour.

The core idea for the brand 'Colour play' was expressed through a custom typeface, 'Colour Milled'. Inspired by piped icing textures, the typeface took the concept of decoration and playfulness and applied it to the bold, condensed sans serif that Universal Favourite had developed for the logo. Initially intended for use as a simple CM monogram, it became clear that a full typeface would be a simple, ownable asset that makes any application immediately recognisable to the brand. The typeface was crafted in uppercase and is used for headlines across all applications. ●

AMA

○ Design: Studio Tempo ○ Web: studiotempo.co ○ Type: PicNic and Helvetica Now.

Studio Tempo's aim was to create a product that captivated children and instilled confidence in parents. They merged modern, appealing design with a playful, personality-filled approach. Packaging was crafted to offer a unique sensory experience during baths. Studio Tempo chose Marielle Nils' 'PicNic' font to embody the brand, its resemblance to shampoo foam serving as a visual metaphor for freshness and naturalness. ●

Dashi

○ Design: Super Studio
○ Web: super-studio.ca
○ Type: Logo—Custom. Other—PP Gosha Sans.

Super Studio crafted this brand design for Dashi, a rapidly growing ramen spot in Trois-Rivières. Opting for a typographic approach, they ensured instant brand recognition with noodles. The logo ingeniously shapes the 'S' in 'Dashi' like a ramen noodle, subtly emphasising the restaurant's focus. Additionally, the logotype features a 'D' reminiscent of a Narutomaki spiral, symbolising authenticity and dynamism. This choice pays homage to traditional ramen ingredients, adding flair and culinary excellence to the design. With these thoughtful touches, Super Studio captured Dashi's essence—vibrant, authentic, and playful—ensuring a lasting impression on customers. ●

'The logo ingeniously shapes the 'S' in 'Dashi' like a ramen noodle, subtly emphasising the restaurant's focus. Additionally, the logotype features a 'D' reminiscent of a Narutomaki spiral, symbolising authenticity and dynamism.'

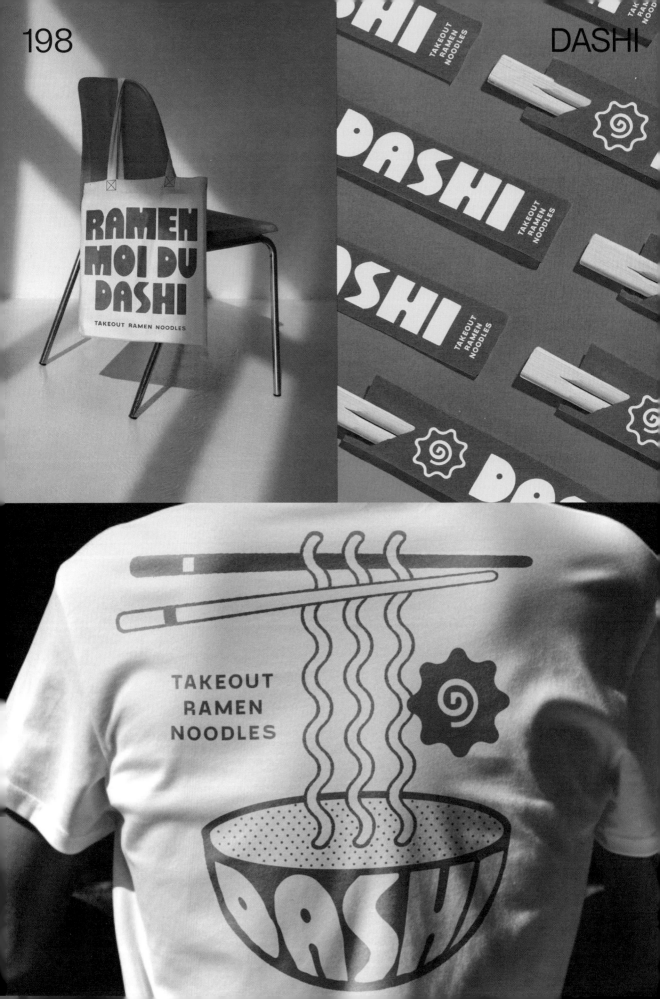

Expressive Type

Counter-Print: © 2024
○ counter-print.co.uk
○ info@counter-print.co.uk

ISBN: 978-1-915392-13-8
Design: Edited and designed by Counter-Print.

Primary Typeface:
○ Lay Grotesk

Cover Typefaces:
○ Clay
○ Aerobik
○ ED Daffodil
○ Superficial
○ Flowstate
○ Rotonto
○ V1OLET
○ Module
○ Rabbit Hole

Printing and Binding: 1010 Printing International Limited, China.

First published in the United Kingdom in 2024.

British Library cataloguing-in-publication data:
A catalogue of this book can be found in the British Library.